MAGIC AND ILLUSIONS

by Tim Cooke

Crabtree Publishing Company
www.crabtreebooks.com

Crabtree Publishing Company
www.crabtreebooks.com

Author: Tim Cooke
Designer: Lynne Lennon
Picture Researcher: Andrew Webb
Picture Manager: Sophie Mortimer
Art Director: Keith Davis
Editorial Director: Lindsey Lowe
Children's Publisher: Anne O'Daly
Editor: Kelly Spence
Proofreader: Kathy Middleton
Cover Design: Margaret Amy Salter
Production Coordinator and
    Prepress Technician: Ken Wright
Print Coordinator: Margaret Amy Salter

Photographs
Cover: Shutterstock
Interior: Alamy: Everett Collection 17; Dreamstime: 5, 21, Josef Sedmak 15; Getty Images: Apic 4, Rosie Hallam/Barcroft Media 11, Chris Hondros/Newsmakers 11; Library of Congress: 16; Mary Evans Picture Library: 20; Shutterstock: 10, 18, 25, S. Buckley 22, Alessandro Collee 13, Simone Conti 23, Everett Collection 27, Fotovika 8, Galich Studio 26, Margo Harrison 29, Steve Heap 12, Antonio Petrone 28, Chris Rawlins 14; SuperStock: Reel FX Creative Studios/Album 7; Thinkstock: Richard Georg 6, iStockphoto 24.

Every attempt to contact copyright holders has been made by the publisher.

Library and Archives Canada Cataloguing in Publication

Cooke, Tim, 1961-, author
    Magic and illusions / Tim Cooke.

(Mystery files)
Includes index.
Issued in print and electronic formats.
ISBN 978-0-7787-8072-4 (bound).--ISBN 978-0-7787-8076-2 (pbk.).--
ISBN 978-1-4271-9969-0 (pdf).--ISBN 978-1-4271-9965-2 (html)

    1. Tricks--Juvenile literature. I. Title.

GV1548.C65 2015   j793.8   C2014-908107-3
                                     C2014-908108-1

Library of Congress Cataloging-in-Publication Data

CIP available at the Library of Congress

Crabtree Publishing Company
www.crabtreebooks.com   1-800-387-7650

Published in Canada
Crabtree Publishing
616 Welland Ave.
St. Catharines, ON
L2M 5V6

Published in the United States
Crabtree Publishing
PMB 59051
350 Fifth Avenue, 59th Floor
New York, New York 10118

Published by **CRABTREE PUBLISHING COMPANY in 2015**
Copyright © 2015 Brown Bear Books Ltd

Printed in Canada/022015/MA20150101

Contents

Introduction

HOUDINI

PRESENTS HIS OWN ORIGINAL INVENTION THE GREATEST SENSATIONAL MYSTERY EVER ATTEMPTED IN THIS OR ANY OTHER AGE!!!

£200 REWARD TO ANY ONE PROVING THAT IT IS POSSIBLE TO OBTAIN AIR IN THE UP-SIDE-DOWN POSITION IN WHICH HOUDINI RELEASES HIMSELF FROM THIS WATER-FILLED-TORTURE-CELL.

Do you believe in magic? Your answer might depend on what you think magic is. In the past, people believed magic was a **supernatural** power. Magic influenced their lives to explain things that could not be explained. Magicians appeared to connect daily life with the mysterious world of gods and spirits.

World of Illusion

Today, most people think of magicians as entertainers on stage or on TV. Their tricks are often spectacular, but the audience always knows there is an explanation behind each trick—they just can't figure out what it is!

Harry Houdini was one of the most famous magicians of all time.

4

Over hundreds of years, magicians and their tricks have grown more imaginative and daring. From basic card tricks to high-flying stunts, tricks continue to amaze and puzzle audiences.

This book explores different magic tricks and illusions and explains possible ways they are performed. But it also looks at other kinds of magic, such as religious **miracles** and the incredible feats of people who can do amazing things that seem like the work of magic.

Sawing a person IN HALF

In 1921, the British magician Selbit performed an astounding trick. He appeared to saw a woman completely in half. Almost one hundred years later, the illusion is still amazing audiences.

Selbit asked his female assistant to climb into a long, wooden box. He tied her arms and legs and closed the lid. He sawed through the middle of the box with a large handsaw. It looked as though he was sawing his assistant in half through her waist. When he opened the box, however, she was still lying with the ropes attached to her arms and legs, and she was unharmed.

The use of saws adds an exciting element of danger to the illusion.

Mystery words...

illusion: something that seems real but is not

6

The illusion was a hit. Other magicians copied Selbit, adding their own details such as holes for their arms and legs to stick out of the box.

How Is It Done?

All versions of the illusion depend on the magician's assistant being very flexible. During the sawing, he or she tucks her legs under her body, and pokes false feet out of the end of the box. She sticks her legs straight out again just before the box is opened.

The magician's assistant folds back her legs inside the box.

Frozen in ICE

On November 27, 2000, American illusionist David Blaine was sealed inside a block of solid ice in Times Square, New York City. After an incredible 63 hours, 42 minutes, and 14 seconds, he was cut out.

Thousands of people braved the pouring winter rain to witness David Blaine's incredible stunt. After he was finally cut out, Blaine was wobbly and unable to speak. While inside the ice he drank hot tea through one tube, and used another to breathe through.

Blaine had practiced for months to train his mind and body to get used to cold temperatures. For almost three days, he stood locked in the icy chamber. A lack of food made him unsteady on his feet once he was freed from the ice.

For most people, being trapped in ice would mean certain death.

Mystery words...

mystic: someone who claims a closeness with god or the divine world

David Blaine only put on one extra shirt that was tied around his waist.

In India, **mystic** men buried themselves alive to prove their special powers. However, they also used tricks to avoid suffocating. They would use a coffin with a false bottom and dig a tunnel to escape. Mind control alone could not keep them alive.

Staying Alive

People wondered how Blaine had avoided hypothermia. Hypothermia is when the body goes into shock when its temperature falls below 95°F (35°C). It helped that the ice block did not touch most of his body. This also helped prevent frostbite, which is when parts of the body freeze. Another theory for his survival is that he mentally concentrated on not letting his body become too cold.

Walking on WATER

In the Bible, Jesus Christ performed a miracle by walking on water to inspire faith. In 2011, British illusionist Dynamo astonished people when he appeared to walk on the surface of the Thames River in London, England.

A water bug rests on top of a pond thanks to **surface tension**.

It was a warm, summer evening when Dynamo (Steven Frayne) took his first steps on the water—and kept walking. Astonished spectators gathered on nearby Westminster Bridge to watch. As Dynamo continued toward the middle of the river, two kayaks passed nearby. Dynamo journeyed about 100 yards (91 meters) before a police boat arrived and picked him up. Had the illusionist really walked on water?

Mystery words...

surface tension: a film created on the surface of a liquid

A Modern Miracle?

No, he had not. Some people believe Dynamo had actually stepped onto a clear platform just beneath the surface of the water. The passing kayaks were part of the illusion. They seemed to prove that Dynamo was not connected to any supports. But kayaks have shallow bottoms. They could have floated above the submerged platform. The "police" in the boat were most likely actors, too.

People may not be able to walk on water, but some animals can. Some insects can be carried by the surface tension of water. This acts as a kind of film, or layer, on the water. The film can support light weights without breaking.

Dynamo is shown walking on the Thames River outside the Houses of Parliament in London, England.

LEVITATION

There are many stories in religious books about people raising their bodies up into the air. The ability to levitate was believed to show the miraculous nature of divine faith.

In the 19th century, magicians used levitation to create spectacular stage acts. Howard Thurston was the most popular magician in the United States between 1908 and 1936. On stage, he levitated his assistant Princess Karnac while reciting "prayers." While floating, he would pass a hoop around her body to show no wires were being used.

Whole-body levitation is often featured in horror movies.

In 1936 an Indian **yogi** spent four minutes suspended in the air while in a **trance**. His hand rested on a walking stick. His followers thought his levitation was proof of his spiritual power. Critics argued that the stick had somehow supported him.

There are two common types of levitation. In Balducci levitation, the magician appears to rise a few inches off the ground. In whole-body levitation, a person rises off a horizontal surface and hovers in midair.

Tricks of the Trade

Both types of levitation rely on tricks. In Balducci levitation, the audience must only be able to see one of the magician's feet. He lifts that foot off the ground. The other foot appears to lift, but is actually only half-raised. It supports the magician's body. In a whole-body levitation, the person is raised up by a number of concealed wires or hidden supports.

Street performers stage a modern version of levitation.

yogi: an Indian expert in yoga and meditation

13

MIRACLES

People often claim that events that can't be explained by science are "miracles." Most religions use miracles to prove the existence of a deity, or divine being, and inspire faith.

The Bible is full of stories of Jesus Christ performing miracles. The greatest miracle was Jesus rising from the dead after his death on the cross. The Quran, Islam's holy book, describes miracles as supernatural help in everyday life. Many Buddhist religious sites, such as the Somawathie Stupa in Sri Lanka, are associated with miracles, such as the curing of the sick. These sites become destinations of **pilgrimage**.

The religious teacher, Buddha, is said to have left miraculous footprints as he walked.

Complex Explanations

Miracles can be described as any events that do not have a **rational** explanation. Some miracles might be put down to chance—such as when someone recovers from a dangerous illness against all the odds.

Often, people prefer to overlook any possible rational explanation for such events. This suggests that people are attracted to the idea that miracles might actually happen.

Something that is a "one-in-a-million chance" sounds miraculous. But some mathematicians argue that given the size of the world population, "one-in-a-million" events happen often without people noticing anything out of the ordinary.

In one miracle, Jesus Christ filled fishermen's empty nets with fish.

ESCAPOLOGY

Hungarian-American Ehrich Weisz (1874-1926), better known as Harry Houdini, was called the "Handcuff King." He could escape from just about anything: handcuffs, straitjackets, even locked boxes. His tricks made him the most famous magician of all time.

Houdini used hidden **picks** to unlock handcuffs and leg irons.

Houdini's most famous trick was the "Chinese Water Torture Cell." In the trick, Houdini's feet were locked into wooden stocks. He was lowered upside down into a tank of water and had to escape before he drowned. He always made it out in two minutes-- or less!

Houdini is lowered into the "Chinese Water Torture Cell."

Houdini worked for a locksmith and learned that he could open any lock by using duplicate keys or tiny picks made from bent wire. He only needed to conceal, or hide, a handful of keys or picks to be able to escape.

A Showman

Houdini loved to worry his audience. Although he was able to free himself from a lock very quickly, he liked to create suspense. He only broke free at the very last moment, when his audience thought he had failed and must be dead.

Mystery words...

pick: a sharp, bent piece of wire used to open a lock

All in the CARDS

A pack of playing cards is all most magicians need to put on a show. Famous magicians throughout history have amazed audiences with card tricks. It is also the way most beginners start out in magic.

There are hundreds of different card tricks. Some of the most popular are based on the magician guessing the card a member of the audience has picked from the deck. Card tricks demand great skill, because everything can be seen.

Magicians practice special movements known as **sleights of hand**. These movements allow them to switch or hide a card without the audience noticing.

Mystery words...

misdirection: getting an audience to focus on one thing so they miss something else

Making the Trick Work

Card tricks do not rely only on sleight of hand. Magicians can influence people to choose a certain card from a deck. They may put a card in a position that catches the eye so a person will pick that card. Magicians also use cards of varying sizes. This makes them easier to move around. Some cards have tiny markings on the backs or sides to identify them. Magicians might also use equipment like a steel-sprung attachment under a card table that gives them cards when they need them. They might also use a special arm rod, a device that conceals cards up the sleeve.

Mystery File:
QUICK HANDS

Sleights of hand are essential for card tricks. These are hand gestures that seem normal but are so quick and skilled that the audience cannot see what is happening. A magician may also use **misdirection** to get the audience to look in the wrong place at a key moment.

It takes hours of training to be able to handle cards well.

SÉANCES

In the 1850s, communicating with dead loved ones through people called spiritualists became popular. At meetings known as séances, the dead spoke through a go-between called a medium.

Séances became a craze that lasted until around 1920. During a séance, the medium sat with a living person in a dark room. The medium called out to a dead relative of the person. The spirit of the dead person appeared to answer. It "spoke" through the medium, or by other signs. These signs might include tapping on a table, or spelling out messages on a **ouija board**. People paid mediums a lot of money for a séance. Trickery was widespread.

At some séances, furniture seemed to move or rise into the air.

The spirit usually "said" just what the listener wanted to hear.

The Fox Sisters

The Fox Sisters of New York claimed to communicate with the spirits through a series of "rappings." They later admitted it was all staged. A helper told them when to make the raps. The sisters pretended spirits were present by cracking joints in their toes and legs.

Harry Houdini believed that all séances were tricks. He was angry that mediums claimed to have special powers. He showed they were fake. He held his own "séances," then revealed the tricks he had used to achieve the same effects as so-called "real" mediums.

A ouija board was a way for spirits to communicate by spelling out words.

Mystery words...

ouija board: a board on which a pointer spells out messages at a séance

21

The Statue of Liberty
VANISHES

On April 8, 1983, the Statue of Liberty vanished. The illusionist David Copperfield made the famous monument disappear in front of a live audience on Liberty Island in New York, and a TV audience of millions. He then made it reappear.

David Copperfield is one of the world's most famous illusionists.

Clearly, it was all an illusion. The statue weighs around 225 tons (228 tonnes) and cannot be moved. Copperfield's spectacular stunt was all carefully **choreographed**. The live audience and the TV cameras were positioned on a platform at an angle in front of two scaffolding towers. The towers framed the statue, which had two rings of very bright lights around its base. The towers held a huge curtain that was drawn in front of the statue. When the curtain was pulled back, the statue was gone. Searchlight beams now illuminated the empty space where the statue had stood just moments before.

Mystery words...

choreographed: planned in a series of steps, like a dance

David Copperfield is known for spectacular stunts, such as walking through the Great Wall of China. One of his most spectacular illusions is known as Portal. He appears to transport himself and a member of the audience from a TV studio to Hawaii.

The Statue of Liberty is so huge it could never have been moved.

Where Did It Go?

So, where was the statue? The answer was simple: it was where it had always been. When the curtain closed, the platform holding the audience and the TV cameras turned, too slowly for anyone to notice. By the time the curtain opened, one of the towers now stood between the audience and the statue, so it could not be seen. When the curtain closed and re-opened, the platform had turned back to its original position and the statue was once again visible.

Magical MEMORY

Some people have exceptional memories. Their powers seem to be magical. In fact, people have long understood that it is possible to train the mind to achieve spectacular feats of memory. Memory magicians use these skills to amaze and entertain.

One way of improving the memory is to link things you want to remember to places.

The loci method is a **visualization** technique that was invented by the ancient Greeks to improve the memory. You must imagine that the things you need to remember have been put in physical places. This makes it easier to remember more information.

3.141592653589793238462.

The value of pi is a favorite subject for memory experts.

Memory masters train their brains in different techniques so they can remember huge amounts of detailed information. Some can recite the value of pi (the ratio of a circle's circumference to its diameter) to over 65,000 figures after the decimal point. One man memorized the sequence of 520 shuffled playing cards.

Training the Brain

Some people who remember a lot of information develop a large hippocampus, the part of the brain that deals with memory. Some people who have a medical condition known as autism also have remarkable memories. Kim Peek, who inspired the movie *Rain Man* (1988), remembered 12,000 books word for word.

Mystery words...

visualization: the process of forming images in the mind

Dangerous
WEAPONS

Magicians have often used weapons to add risk and excitement to their acts. Throwing knives, shooting arrows, and even dodging bullets are all standard tricks. They require the magician and the assistant to use all kinds of techniques.

Probably the most dangerous of all magic tricks is the bullet-catch trick. In this illusion, a loaded gun is fired directly at the face of the magician. The magician then appears to catch the moving bullet between his teeth. The trick is almost as old as guns themselves. It was first performed in the 16th century. At least 15 magicians died attempting this trick.

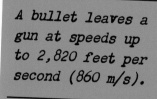

A bullet leaves a gun at speeds up to 2,820 feet per second (860 m/s).

Penn and Teller

The American magicians Penn and Teller have made the bullet-catch their **showstopper**. Facing each other, they fire a gun at the same time through a pane of glass. Both catch a bullet in their teeth. The bullets are signed by members of the audience beforehand, but the magicians use sleight of hand to replace the real bullets with wax ones that are fired. They use misdirection so they have time to place the signed bullets in their mouths and get rid of the wax bullets.

Mystery File:
KNIFE-THROWING

Knife-throwing and archery displays have been part of the circus or magic shows for hundreds of years. Magicians need a steady hand and a blunt knife tip. They also need a flexible partner who can bend out of the way of stray blades.

Mystery words...

showstopper: part of a performance that receives prolonged applause

27

Sword-
SWALLOWING

Watching performers put long, sharp swords down their throats makes most people squirm. Magicians train themselves to swallow any kind of long object, such as pool cues and drumsticks. But sword-swallowing is not an illusion. It is real—and extremely dangerous!

I n this act the performer actually swallows the sword or other object. Mastering this skill requires hours of practice.

Gag Reflex

When you put something in your mouth other than food or drink, your body rejects it by **gagging**. This closes the muscles at the top of the throat. The first step for a sword-swallower is to learn to control his or her gag reflex. Once he or she has overcome this, the

A sword-swallower tilts his head to help relax the muscles of his gut.

Monsieur Mangetout once ate an entire Cessna light airplane.

performer has to learn how to pass a solid piece of metal down the throat without causing damage.

Muscle Control

When food passes down the throat, the muscles squeeze and contract to push it toward the stomach. When a sword passes through, the muscles have to be relaxed. A magician will spend years training his or her muscles. If the muscles contract, the sword's blade will cut into the muscle fiber, and the magician could bleed to death. That is why a sword-swallower always tips his or her head back. This signals to "warn" the muscles what is about to happen. It sounds easy, but it isn't! It can kill an inexperienced person.

Mystery File: BON APPETIT

The body can be trained to eat many things. The French performer Monsieur Mangetout ("Mr. Eats Everything") ate rubber, glass, and metal. He broke objects such as bicycles down into small pieces and washed them down with fluid.

Mystery words...

gagging: the involuntary closing of the throat by the body

Glossary

choreographed Planned in a series of steps, like a dance

divine Related to a god or gods

escapology The branch of magic involving escaping from restraints such as handcuffs

gagging The involuntary closing of the throat by the body

illusion Something that seems real but is not

illusionist A magician who performs illusions

levitation The act of raising a person or object into the air by supernatural means

miracles Events that are seen as the result of divine action

misdirection Getting an audience to focus on one thing so they miss something else

mystic Someone who claims to be close to god or the divine world

ouija board A board on which a pointer spells out messages at a séance

pick A sharp, bent piece of wire used to open a lock

pilgrimage A journey made to a holy site for a religious purpose

rational Describes something that can be explained by reason or logic

showstopper Part of a performance that receives prolonged applause

sleights of hand Movements that are so rapid they cannot be accurately observed

supernatural Something that is caused by forces beyond scientific explanation

surface tension A supportive film on the surface of a liquid

trance A semi-conscious state in which a person is not aware of what is around them

visualization The process of forming images in the mind

yogi An Indian expert in yoga and meditation

Find Out More

BOOKS

Bednar, Chuck. *David Blaine: Illusionist and Endurance Artist* (Transcending Race in America). Mason Crest, 2009.

Hill. Douglas. *Witches and Magic Makers* (Eyewitness). Dorling Kindersley, 2000.

Piehl, Janet. *Harry Houdini* (History Maker Bios). Lerner Publications, 2009.

Price, Sean Stewart. *Vanished! Magic Tricks and Great Escapes* (Culture in Action). Raintree, 2010.

Sherman, Patrice. *The Secret, Mystifying, Unusual History of Magic* (Unusual Histories). Capstone Press, 2010.

WEBSITES

History of Magic
A detailed, free documentary about the history of magic from earliest times until today.
http://topdocumentaryfilms.com/history-of-magic/

Ten Magicians
The British newspaper *The Guardian* lists its all-time greatest magicians, with details of their tricks.
www.theguardian.com/culture/gallery/2013/may/04/the-10-best-magicians

Try It Yourself
Download PDFs with instructions on magic tricks for kids.
http://magictricksforkids.org/

Index

BACK
ROADS
OF
TEXAS

Hill country swine

approaching Doss, Gillespie County

Back Roads of Texas
by Earl Thollander

NORTHLAND PRESS FLAGSTAFF, ARIZONA

Panna Maria, Karnes County

Front cover ... Lange Mill near Doss,
Gillespie County

Books by Earl Thollander
BACK ROADS OF ARIZONA
BACK ROADS OF CALIFORNIA
BACK ROADS OF OREGON
BACK ROADS OF NEW ENGLAND
BARNS OF CALIFORNIA

to my back
road companions,
Joe and Wes

Contents

The Hill Country of Central Texas

Bulls, King Ranch near Kingsville

West of Houston and East of San Antonio

Southwest Texas and the Big Bend Country

Southern Texas along the Rio Grande to the Gulf of Mexico

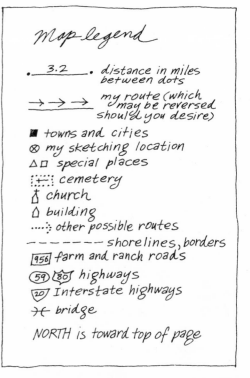

map legend

. 3.2 . distance in miles between dots

→ → → my route (which may be reversed should you desire)

■ towns and cities
⊗ my sketching location
△□ special places
cemetery
church
building
other possible routes
– – – – – shorelines, borders
956 farm and ranch roads
59 80 highways
20 Interstate highways
)(bridge

NORTH is toward top of page

Preface

    In this book I have tried to capture the flavor of the rural landscape, the small town, the beauty, and some of the humor to be found on the back roads of Texas. For the most part I've given cities a wide berth in order to escape their influence, for I enjoy the more local, slower-paced communities of humankind.

    It is also fascinating to me to find contact with Texas history through its architecture, from log cabin to county courthouse, and to quietly contemplate the Texans who built and used it.

    Undisturbed nature is becoming more difficult to find, but on the back roads I see it in the flight of birds, in free flowing streams, in trees, mountains and canyons, and in the sky. These fill my being with a profound love of life.

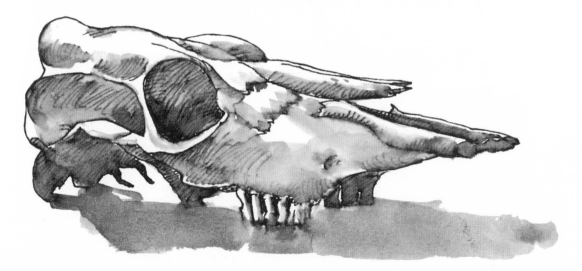

Desert
Marigold

Author's Note

The six parts of BACK ROADS OF TEXAS each have a sectional map to show generally where the back roads are. These sectional areas can be easily located on a state map that is available from Texas tourist bureaus, automobile clubs, chambers of commerce, and other travel services. The local maps that I have made for each back road should then guide you accurately on your way. Arrows point the direction in which I traveled, but trips can easily be reversed should you so desire. The north pole is toward the top of each map. Maps are not the same in scale due to the great diversity in distances traveled. Instead, I have made mileage notations for each route. County maps may be obtained at nominal cost by writing to the State Department of Highways and Public Transportation, Transportation Planning Division, P.O. Box 5051, Austin, Texas 78763.

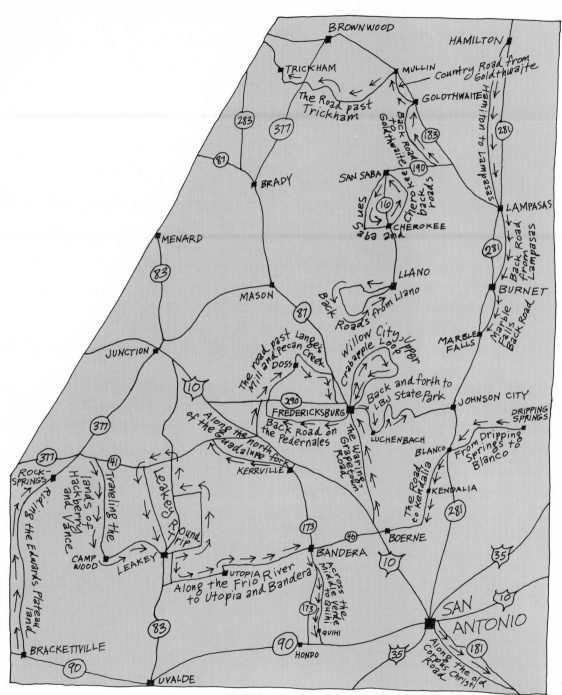

BROWNWOOD

HAMILTON

TRICKHAM

MULLIN

Country Road from
Goldthwaite

The Road past
Trickham

GOLDTHWAITE

283

377

Back Road to
Goldthwaite

Hamilton to Lampasas

281

81

BRADY

SAN SABA

183

190

Cherokee back roads

LAMPASAS

16

CHEROKEE

San Saba and

281

MENARD

Back Road from Lampasas

83

LLANO

Back Roads from Llano

BURNET

Marble Falls Back Road

MASON

81

Willow City, Upper Crabapple Loop

MARBLE FALLS

JUNCTION

The road past Lange's Mill and Pecan Creek

DOSS

Back and forth to LBJ State Park

JOHNSON CITY

10

290

FREDERICKSBURG

DRIPPING SPRINGS

377

Along the north fork of the Guadalupe

Back Road on the Pedernales

The Waring? Road

LUCHENBACH

From Dripping Springs to Blanco

377

41

KERRVILLE

BLANCO

ROCK-SPRINGS

Traveling the lands of Hackberry and Vance

Leakey Round Trip

The Road to Kendalia

KENDALIA

281

Riding the Edwards Plateau land

CAMP WOOD

LEAKEY

UTOPIA

Along the Frio River to Utopia and Bandera

173

BANDERA

Across the Middle Verde to Quihi

46

BOERNE

10

35

SAN ANTONIO

10

83

173

QUIHI

35

Along the old Corpus Christi Road

181

BRACKETTVILLE

90

90

HONDO

UVALDE

12

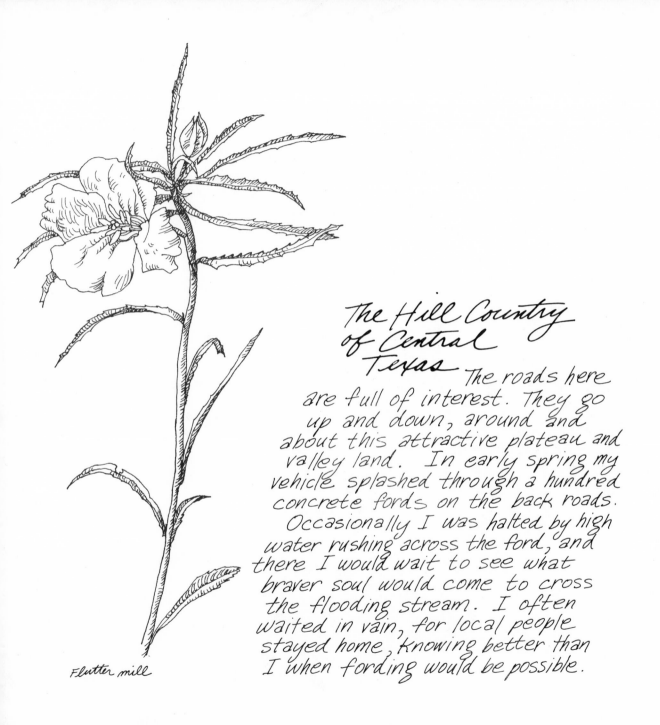

Flutter mill

The Hill Country of Central Texas

The roads here are full of interest. They go up and down, around and about this attractive plateau and valley land. In early spring my vehicle splashed through a hundred concrete fords on the back roads. Occasionally I was halted by high water rushing across the ford, and there I would wait to see what braver soul would come to cross the flooding stream. I often waited in vain, for local people stayed home, knowing better than I when fording would be possible.

Leakey round trip

Through rocky gorges glistening
from the previous night's rain, Farm Road 337 achieved
some height on this hill country trip from Leakey.
Oaks were just budding pink, reddish,
and orange, and an occasional redbud bloomed
bright purple against a dark juniper.

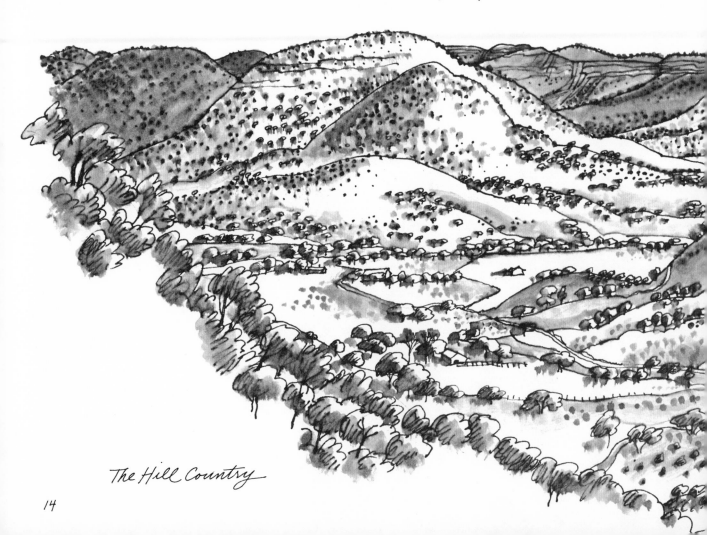

The Hill Country

At the crest was this view of the hills
dotted with oaks, ponds shimmering in
the sun, and cows placidly grazing.
    Along the rolling plateau of Road 187,
oak forests and juniper grew on land so strewn
with rocks it appeared to be a mosaic design.

There is intense pastoral beauty along Road 336, with its neatly cropped pasture land. I came across cows lying on the road and a Black Angus running ahead with her calf. After I sorted my way through these, a deer leaped a fence to the right, flashing a luxuriant white tail. On my left flew a big grey heron.

At the site of the McLauren Massacre, April 19, 1881, the last Indian raid in Frio Canyon, is a marker telling the story. Here, near the West Frio River, I sketched Texas pecan trees and an old farmhouse on the Knippa ranch. A cowpuncher who had once lived in the house opened the gate for me so I could move to a closer view.

Cabin near the site of the McLauren Massacre

17

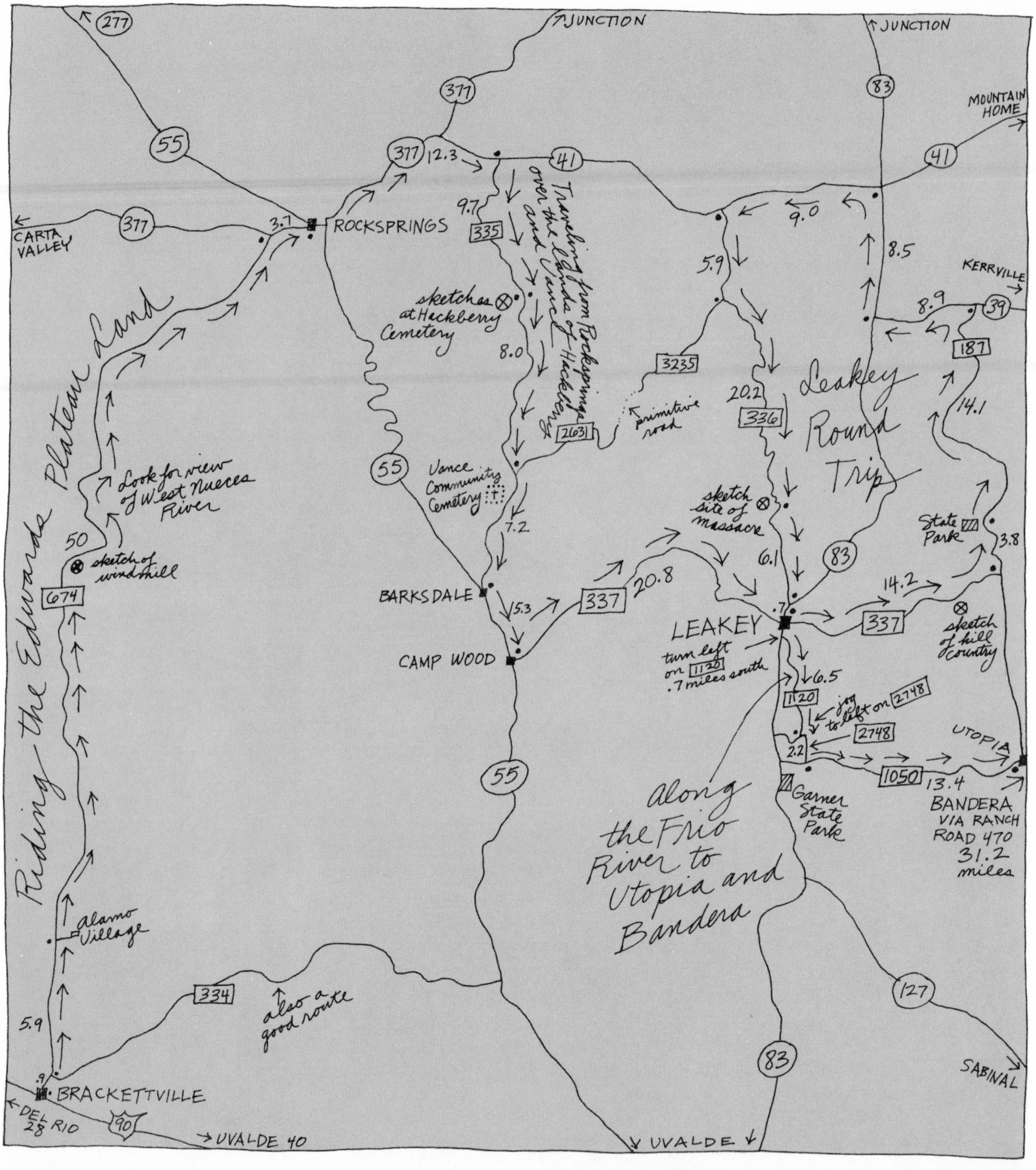

277
JUNCTION
JUNCTION
377
83
55
MOUNTAIN HOME
377
12.3
41
41
CARTA VALLEY
377
3.7
ROCKSPRINGS
9.7
335
Traveling from Rocksprings over the lands of Hackberry and Vance
9.0
5.9
8.5
KERRVILLE
8.9
39
sketches at Hackberry Cemetery
187
8.0
3235
Leakey Round Trip
Riding the Edwards Plateau Land
20.2
336
primitive road
14.1
2631
55
Vance Community Cemetery
Look for view of West Nueces River
sketch site of massacre
State Park
7.2
3.8
50
sketch of windmill
6.1
83
674
BARKSDALE
20.8
14.2
5.3
337
.7
LEAKEY
337
sketch of hill country
turn left on 1120 .7 miles south
CAMP WOOD
6.5
1120
jog to left on 2748
2748
UTOPIA
2.2
1050
13.4
55
Garner State Park
BANDERA VIA RANCH ROAD 470 31.2 miles
Along the Frio River to Utopia and Bandera
Alamo Village
334
also a good route
127
5.9
83
.9
SABINAL
BRACKETTVILLE
DEL RIO 28
90
UVALDE 40
UVALDE

Traveling from Rocksprings over the lands of Hackberry and Vance.

My car seemed to bound along in roller coaster fashion on the up and down road paralleling Hackberry Creek!

Hackberry and Vance were early settlements in this area. At a cemetery along the way, community members' graves may be seen.

I sketched Ben Tanner's headstone, admirable in its simplicity, and also Mary Malisa Billings's, with the inscription, "bornd: May 9, 1885."

MARY: MALISA: BILLINGS
WAS: BORND: MAY 9: 1885
AND: DIED · 14 DAY: OF
APRIL 1887.

BEN. T.

BEN TANNER

Riding the Edwards Plateau land

This was the road I first traveled on into the Hill Country. Outside of Brackettville, once the supply town for old Fort Clark, I passed Alamo Village, site of the John Wayne movie of 1959, "The Alamo."

Yuccas were blooming and trees beginning to leaf. The landscape was park-like, and among groves of oaks and juniper one might see wild turkeys. Herds of Angora goats grazed, Rocksprings being a center for this industry.

Along the road to Rocksprings

Along the Frio River to Utopia and Bandera

There were views of the river and the big trees on its banks. Several tortoises in the road had to be avoided. Because they look like rocks, the passing cars skirt them, and so the tortoises are safer than the poor armadillo, whose fate made him nocturnal and not so easily seen. Mashed armadillo is a sad sight to us on the roadways, although a welcome one to the Texas buzzard.

I sketched Bandera's silver-towered 1890 courthouse. It looms high over the little town. A historical marker notes the fact that B.F. Trester of San Antonio drew the courthouse plans for a fee of five dollars.

Bandera County Courthouse

Across the Middle Verde to Quihi

I was impressed by the beauty of Middle
Verde Creek with its green, grassy banks and oaks.
A farmer came along and said, "You wouldn't think
it so pretty if you'd seen it five days ago, when
a storm made it a raging torrent."
I sketched the little hamlet of Quihi with
the red-bricked, white-trimmed
1914 Lutheran Church, still
standing proud.

Middle Verde Creek, Medina County

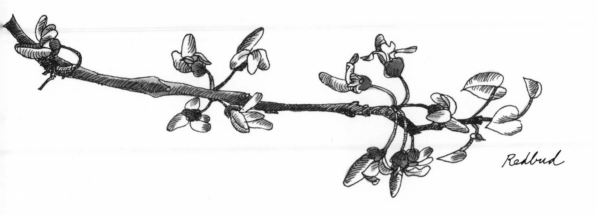

Redbud

Along the north fork of the Guadalupe River

Fancy gates gave entrance to
some elegant ranches along this pleasant
country road. There were many crossings
of the north fork of the Guadalupe
River. In addition to sighting several
wild turkeys, I came across an untethered
llama on this journey.

Stone refuge,
Guadalupe River

27

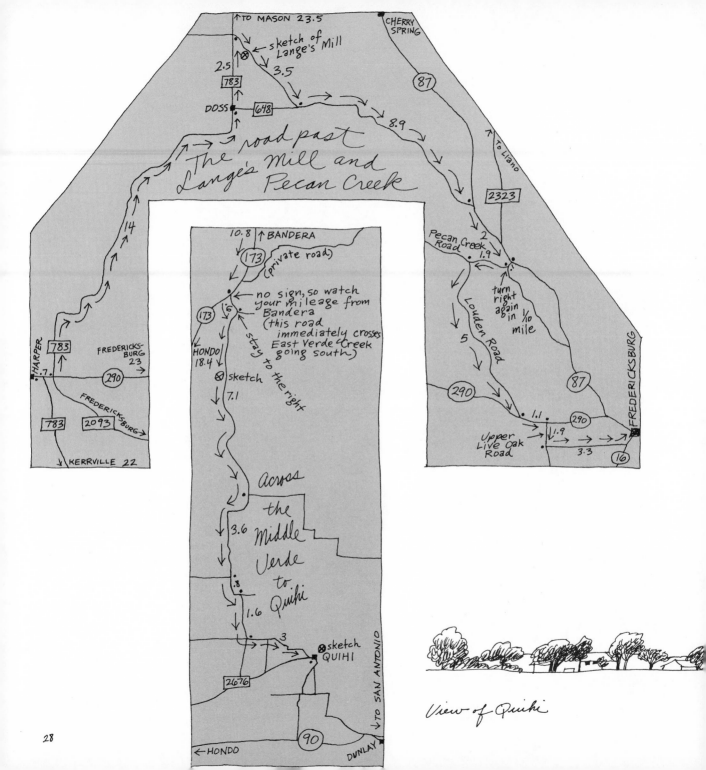

↑TO MASON 23.5

CHERRY SPRING

← sketch of Lange's Mill

3.5

2.5

783

DOSS

648

8.9

87

To Llano

2323

The road past Lange's Mill and Pecan Creek

14

Pecan Creek Road 2

1.9

10.8 ↑BANDERA

173

(private road)

no sign, so watch your mileage from Bandera (this road immediately crosses East Verde Creek going south)

173

.6

turn right again in 1/10 mile

Louden Road

5

HONDO 18.4

sketch

7.1

stay to the right

290

HARPER

783

.7

FREDERICKSBURG 23

290

FREDERICKSBURG

783

2093

FREDERICKSBURG →

KERRVILLE 22

Across the Middle Verde to Quihi

290

1.1

290

Upper Live Oak Road

1.9

3.3

16

FREDERICKSBURG

87

3.6

.8

1.6

.3

sketch QUIHI

2676

←TO SAN ANTONIO

View of Quihi

90

←HONDO

DUNLAY

28

The road past Lange's Mill and Pecan Creek

At Doss you will see directional signs for local farmers listing the names of descendants of the first German settlers. Names included one Strackbein, one Bierschwale, six Gerstweidts, five Andereggs, five Crenwelges, and one Rodrigues.

The church at Doss is the "Evangelisch Lutherisch St. Pedre Gemeinde," 1912.

Lange's Mill was established in 1849 by the Doss brothers. Until 1888 it was operated by Julius Lange. This is private property, but the mill can be viewed from the road. My drawing shows Threadgill Creek in the foreground. In the Pioneer Museum in Fredericksburg can be seen a Lange Mill flour sack and the wooden block from which it was printed.

Lange's Mill

31

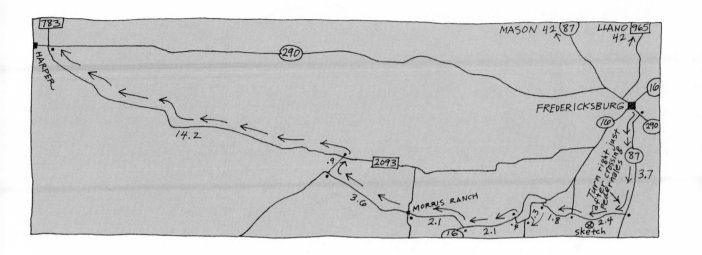

783

HARPER

290

MASON 42 (87)   LLANO 965
                    42

16

FREDERICKSBURG

16   290

87

3.7

Turn right just
after crossing
Pedernales

14.2

2093

.9

3.6

MORRIS RANCH

2.1

16   2.1

1.3

1.8

⊗ 2.4
sketch

Hill Country farm

Back road on the Pedernales

After only a few minutes, one is away
from town and out into the country viewing
crops and venerable German-style stone
farmhouses.
Along this hill country back road
I sketched white Angora goats — dainty,
placid animals with pink noses and
angelic faces.
Next to them, as if in contrast,
was an assorted group of swine,
either snorting or snoring.

Hill Country Angora goats

34

35

Willow City and Upper Crabapple loop from Fredericksburg

I hiked to Balanced Rock following white arrows that pointed the way. It's a bit of a scramble for the one-quarter mile hike — but rewarding. The location affords a good view of the countryside, and the rock really does have astonishing balance. Graffiti on the rock went back as far as 1891. Further along this road, Enchanted Rock State Park encompasses the great pink granite dome that has long been a landmark in this area.

At times the road to Willow City is like driving through private parkland. Watch for cows and calves along the way.

At a higher elevation there are fine stands of yucca and rabbit-ear cactus.

Scarlet Paintbrush

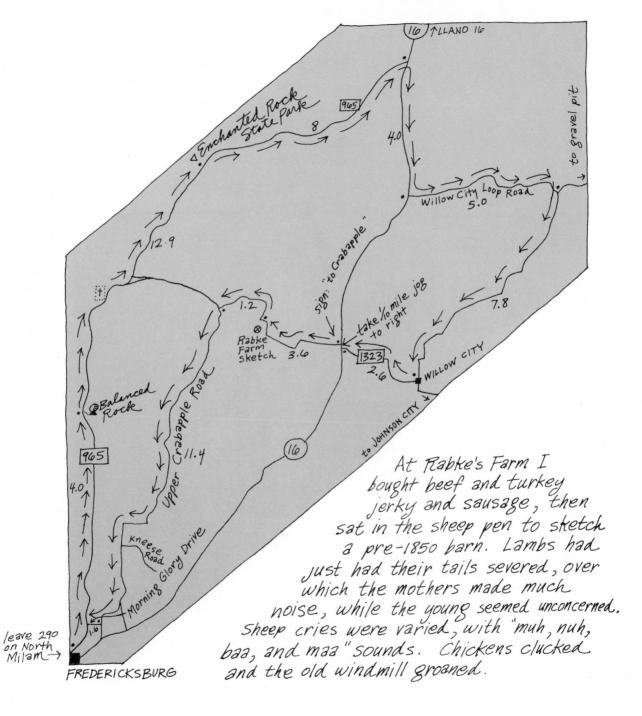

16 ↑LLANO 16

to gravel pit

◊ Enchanted Rock State Park

965

8

4.0

Willow City Loop Road 5.0

12.9

sign: "to Crabapple"

take 1/10 mile jog to right

1.2

⊗ Rabke Farm Sketch 3.6

7.8

✝

965

4.0

@ Balanced Rock

Upper Crabapple Road 11.4

Kneese Road

Morning Glory Drive

16

1323

2.6

■ WILLOW CITY

to JOHNSON CITY

1.6

FREDERICKSBURG

At Rabke's Farm I
bought beef and turkey
jerky and sausage, then
sat in the sheep pen to sketch
a pre-1850 barn. Lambs had
just had their tails severed, over
which the mothers made much
noise, while the young seemed unconcerned.
Sheep cries were varied, with "muh, nuh,
baa, and maa" sounds. Chickens clucked
and the old windmill groaned.

³⁸ Rabke's Farm

39

Back and forth and roundabout
to LBJ State Park

The John Peter Tatsch House at West Schubert and North Bowie in Fredericksburg was built in 1856 by Tatsch, a "Tischler," (cabinetmaker) by trade. He made his fireplace big enough to roast an entire cow. You can see a similar fireplace and many other things of historical interest at the Gillespie County Historical Society's Pioneer Museum, 309 West Main Street.

The Peter Tatsch house

Back roads from Fredericksburg were called
"Peach Blossom Trails of Gillespie County" by the
Chamber of Commerce, a nice, roundabout way
to reach LBJ State Park. I had to ford
the Pedernales along the way.
      I enjoyed viewing the farming
country and stone farmhouses.
      This year, however, the young
            peach orchards experienced
            a March hailstorm, and
               thousands of delicate
               pink blossoms were
               knocked to the
               ground.

Back and forth and roundabout to LBJ State Park

FREDERICKSBURG

1631

1631

631

4.2

2721

1623

LBJ
State
Park

1.8

turn left on
Goehmann Lane

290

6.3

Jung Road

4.9

jog left
3/10 of mile
sign "Blumenthal"

Gellermann Road

4.3

STONEWALL

3.3

1.0

290

1.0

290

turn left
just before
Grape Creek
Crossing

4.2

1376

4.3

sketch of
mailbox

LUCHENBACH
(Site)

1376

Mailbox near Luchenbach

42

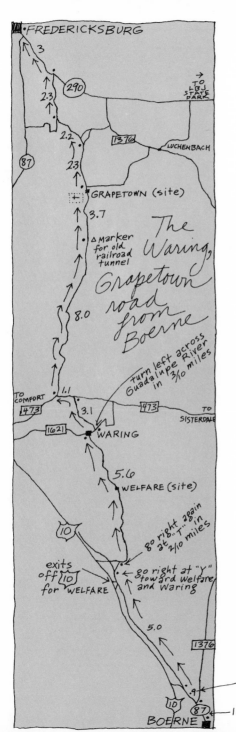

The Waring, Grapetown road from Boerne

In 1887, travelers in these parts forded the Guadalupe River at Waringford. The town had been named in honor of a respected settler, R.P.M. Waring. Postmaster Treiber told me that the present shortened name of the town came about when a black porter on the new railroad line consistently left out the "ford" in his station call.

This was a drive past rolling farmland and old stone farmhouses.

There was a view of Black Creek with clear, blue-green water running over its rocky bed and sheep grazing the bright green banks.

43

Waring Village

45

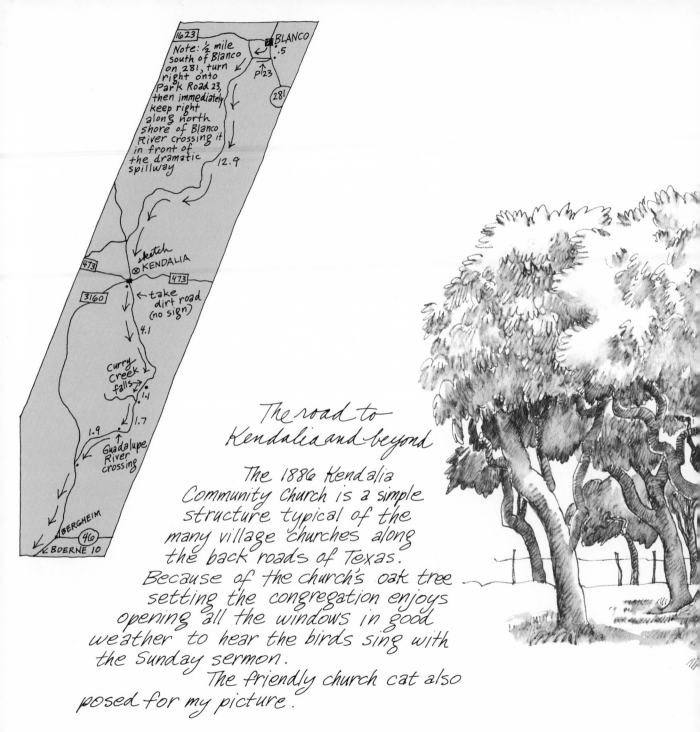

1623

Note: ½ mile south of Blanco on 281, turn right onto Park Road 23, then immediately keep right along north shore of Blanco River crossing it in front of the dramatic spillway

BLANCO
.5

PR23

281

12.9

473

sketch
KENDALIA

473

3160

← take dirt road (no sign)

4.1

Curry Creek falls →

1.1

1.9   1.7

↑
Guadalupe River crossing

BERGHEIM

46

← BOERNE 10

The road to
Kendalia and beyond

The 1886 Kendalia
Community Church is a simple
structure typical of the
many village churches along
the back roads of Texas.
Because of the church's oak tree
setting the congregation enjoys
opening all the windows in good
weather to hear the birds sing with
the Sunday sermon.
        The friendly church cat also
posed for my picture.

Kendalia Community Church

47

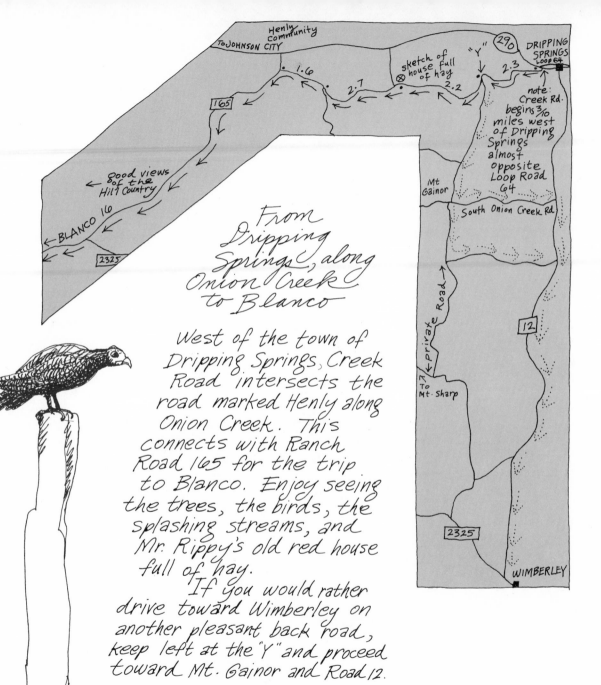

From Dripping Springs, along Onion Creek to Blanco

West of the town of Dripping Springs, Creek Road intersects the road marked Henly along Onion Creek. This connects with Ranch Road 165 for the trip to Blanco. Enjoy seeing the trees, the birds, the splashing streams, and Mr. Rippy's old red house full of hay.

If you would rather drive toward Wimberley on another pleasant back road, keep left at the "Y" and proceed toward Mt. Gainor and Road 12.

Map labels:
Henly Community
To JOHNSON CITY
1.6
2.7
2.2
sketch of house full of hay
"Y"
290
DRIPPING SPRINGS
Loop 64
2.3
note: Creek Rd. begins 3/10 miles west of Dripping Springs almost opposite Loop Road 64
165
good views of the Hill Country
16
BLANCO
2325
Mt Gainor
South Onion Creek Rd.
Private Road
To Mt. Sharp
12
2325
WIMBERLEY

48

House full of hay

Along the old Corpus Christi Highway

This is the pastoral route going south from San Antonio through the little village of Saspamco and across Calaveras Creek on an antiquated steel bridge.

The Misión San Francisco de la Espada is still the parish church for the descendants of the Indian and Spanish converts who continue to live in its environs. Established in 1731, it is the farthest south of San Antonio's five missions. Nearby is a dam, an irrigation ditch, and a fine aqueduct built by the Spaniards.

Evening Primrose

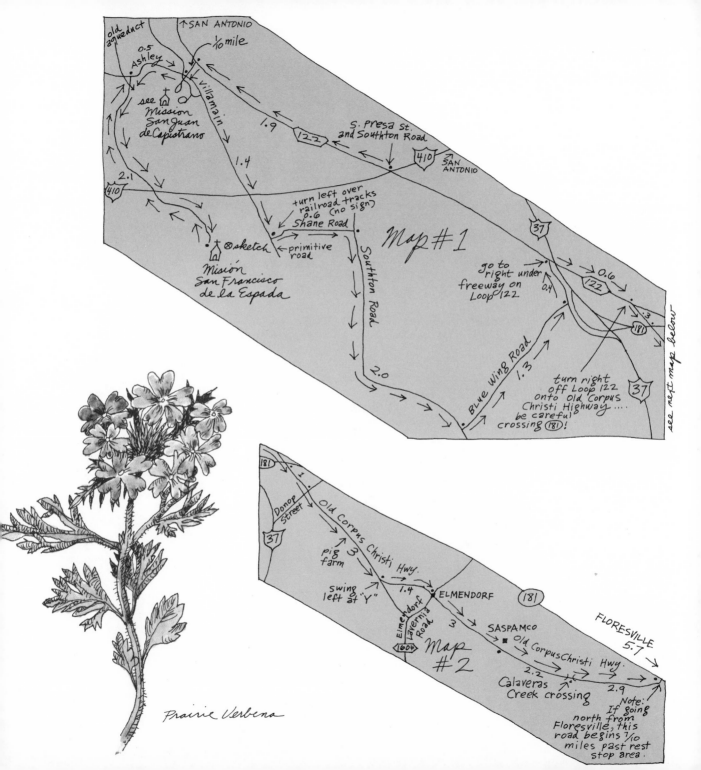

Prairie Verbena

Misión San Francisco
de la Espada, 1756

52

Back roads from Llano

    The Llano River flows right through the town of Llano.
If it is placid enough, you can cross it at Scott's Crossing
to follow dirt roads to Castell. Or you can follow the
pavement on Farm Road 152 to Castell.
    From Castell back to Llano, I forded two
important tributaries of the Llano River, Hickory
and Bullhead creeks, and traveled
through a landscape of
fiercely blooming firewheel
and black-eyed Susan
wildflowers.

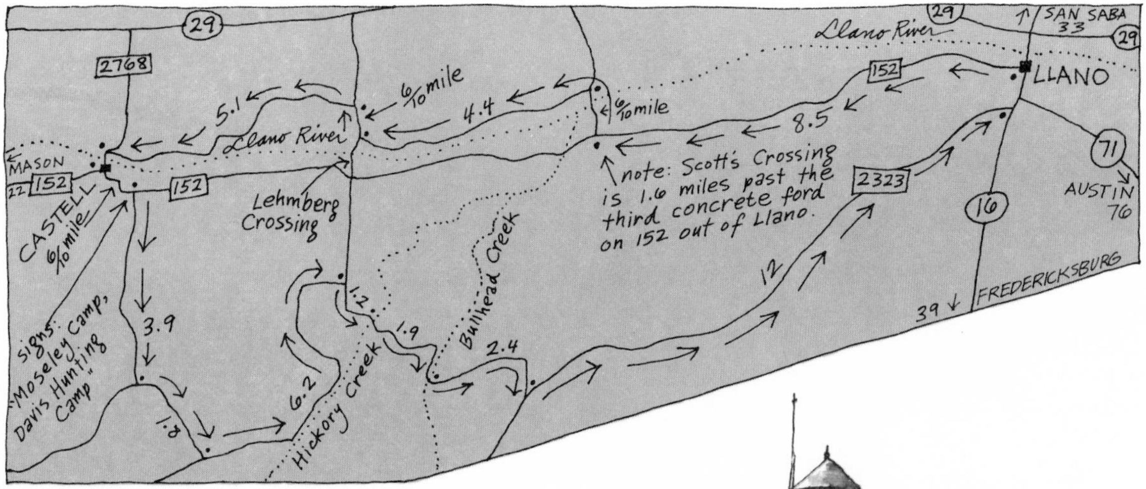
29
2768
Llano River
SAN SABA
33
LLANO
152
6/10 mile
5.1
4.4
8.5
MASON
22
CASTELL
6/10 mile
Lehmberg Crossing
note: Scott's Crossing is 1.6 miles past the third concrete ford on 152 out of Llano.
2323
71
AUSTIN
76
16
FREDERICKSBURG
39
12
Bullhead Creek
Hickory Creek
1.2
1.9
2.4
6.2
3.9
1.8
signs: "Moseley Camp, Davis Hunting Camp"

LLANO

The river flowing past Llano

San Saba and Cherokee back roads

You are lucky if a dirt road route has been recently graded. Otherwise, you must simply slow down to accommodate the bumps! I slowed down on this one. Along the road I saw ponies prancing in a field of white prickly poppies sprinkled with glowing firewheels, big-horned Brahma bulls, fluffy sheep, and buzzards on the road picking at a dead armadillo.

The road out of Cherokee went past several turkey farms. Along Cherokee Creek I stopped to sketch this time-worn log house, still sturdy though perhaps 150 years old.

Log house on Cherokee Creek

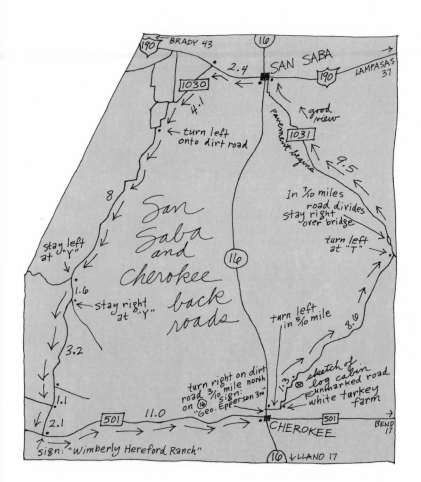

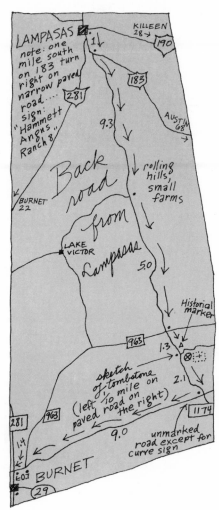

Back road from Lampasas

In 1853 Martha Strickling
and her husband Marmaduke
settled here and began
the community of Strickling,
which once boasted of
having several churches,
a store, and a doctor.
Buffalo hides and
lumber were hauled
through the town, but
when the town was
bypassed by the
railroad, Strickling
languished. Only the
cemetery remains
today, all but
hidden in the
high grass. Birds
sang, leaves rustled,
bees buzzed as my
pen scratched this
remembrance.

ALEY A.
WIFE OF.
A.J.
WADEN
BORN
1824
NOV.
896.

Headstone at Strickling

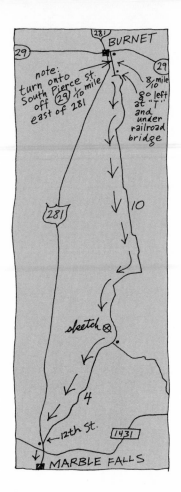

Map labels:
- 281
- BURNET
- 29
- note: turn onto South Pierce St. off 29 1/10 mile east of 281
- 29
- 8/10 mile
- go left at "T" and under railroad bridge
- 281
- 10
- sketch ⊗
- 4
- ←12th St.
- 1431
- MARBLE FALLS

Marble Falls back road

The ford at Hamilton Creek is picturesquely located near the site of an 1850 Mormon settlement and mill.

The concrete ford is a marvelous invention. It puts one in direct contact with creek and stream. The water course is free to rise and fall with the season, yet travel is not restricted unless there is a real downpour. Then the stream is completely in charge and man must wait.

Concrete ford near
Marble Falls

61

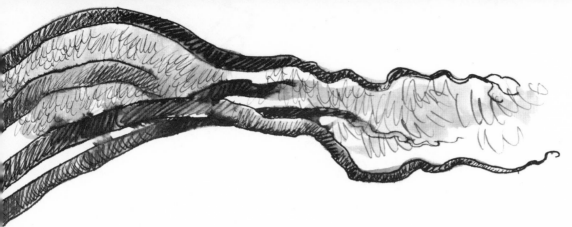

Back road to Goldthwaite

White-tailed deer lept gracefully over fences at my approach. Later I had to drive slowly through large numbers of sheep that congregated on this road. Rams with large curled horns sported brown and black birds on their backs.

I sketched in the shade of a beautiful grove of ash trees.

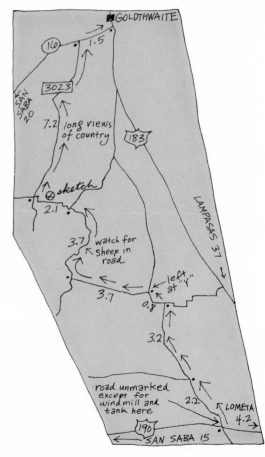

Goldthwaite
16
1.5
3023
SAN SABA 20
7.2 long views of country
183
sketch
2.1
3.7 watch for sheep in road
left at "Y"
3.7
0.8
3.2
LAMPASAS 37
road unmarked except for windmill and tank here
2.2
LOMETA 4.2
190
SAN SABA 15

Back road between Lometa and Goldthwaite

Country road from Goldthwaite

Spring wildflowers bloomed on both sides of this scenic little farm road. At an old stone farmhouse I watched a farmer tending his Angora goats.

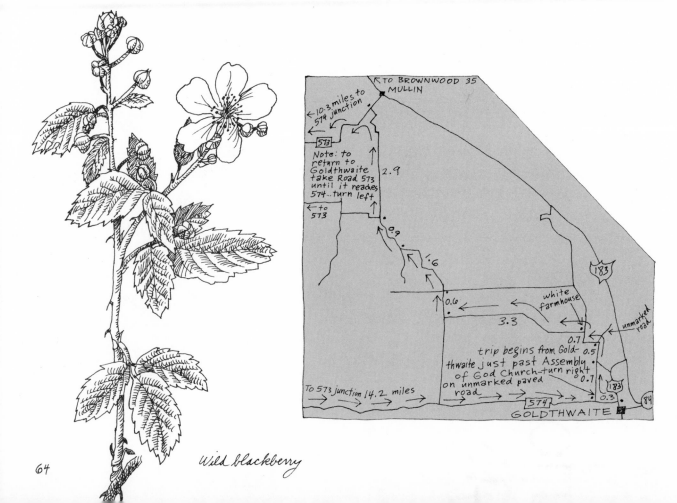

↖ TO BROWNWOOD 35
MULLIN

← 10.3 miles to 574 junction

573

Note: to return to Goldthwaite take Road 573 until it reaches 574...turn left

← to 573

2.9

.9

1.6

0.6

3.3

white farmhouse

183

unmarked road

0.7

0.5

trip begins from Goldthwaite just past Assembly of God Church—turn right on unmarked paved road

0.7

To 573 junction 14.2 miles

574

0.3

183

84

GOLDTHWAITE

Wild blackberry

64

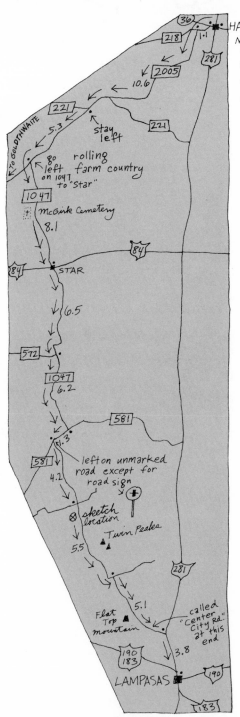

HAMILTON

Note: Go west ½ mile on ③⑥. Turn left on [218] toward Pottsville. In one and 1/10 mile turn left on [2005] toward Goldthwaite.

[36]
[218]
[1-1]
[281]
[2005]
10.6

TO GOLDTHWAITE
[221]
5.3
stay left
[221]

go left on 1047 to "Star"
rolling farm country

[1047]

☩ McGirk Cemetery
8.1

[84]

[84] STAR
6.5

[572]

[1047]
6.2

[581]
1.3

[581]
4.2

left on unmarked road except for road sign

⊗ sketch location

Twin Peaks ▲▲
5.5

[281]

5.1

Flat Top mountain ▲

called "Center City Rd." at this end

3.8

[190]
[183]

LAMPASAS

[190]

[183]

Hamilton to Lampasas

I left Hamilton's pretty, shaded streets and old-fashioned town square, with its townspeople sitting and chatting, and headed south for open country and long scenic views. Spiderwort bloomed deep blue along the road, and there were fields of yellow ragwort and flutter-mill. Flocks of shorn sheep and lambs fed in the green pastureland.

Only the mailman came by as I sketched a view of Twin Peaks and distant Flat Top Mountain. In case you are wondering, the "twin" of Twin Peaks is directly behind the one I drew, so is not in my picture.

On the road to Lampasas

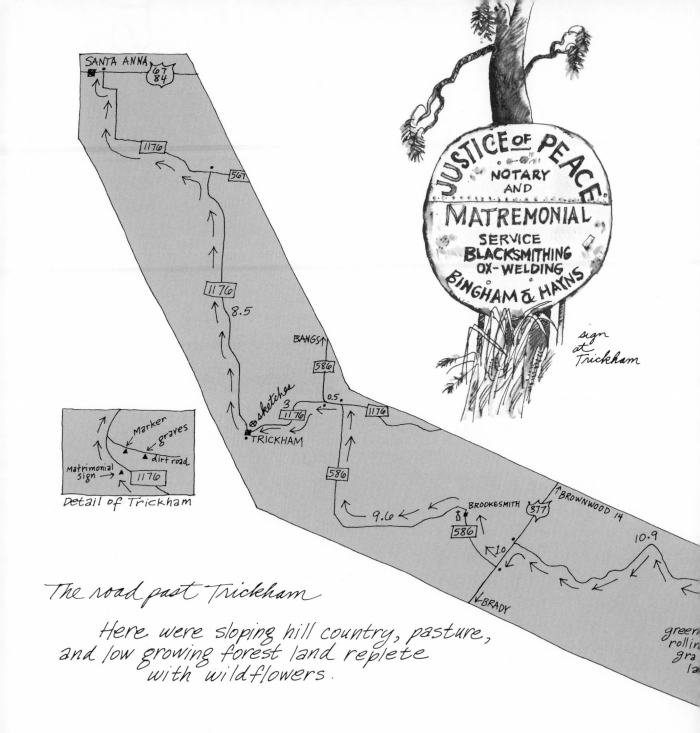

SANTA ANNA
67
84

1176

561

1176

8.5

BANGS

586

sketches
3
1176
0.5
1176

TRICKHAM

586

Marker
graves
dirt road
Matrimonial
sign
1176

Detail of Trickham

9.6

BROOKESMITH
377
BROWNWOOD 14

586
1.0

BRADY

10.9

JUSTICE OF PEACE
· NOTARY ·
AND
MATREMONIAL
SERVICE
BLACKSMITHING
OX-WELDING
BINGHAM & HAYNS

sign
at
Trickham

The road past Trickham

Here were sloping hill country, pasture,
and low growing forest land replete
with wildflowers.

green
rollin
gra
la

old graves at Trickham

At Trickham, the marker near the ancient graves I sketched said, "These unknown pioneers gave their lives in the winning of the frontier. Their names are known only to God." Another marker claimed that because of notorious jokes played at the local general store in this boisterous cowboy community, the name of "Trick-'em" was suggested for the name of the local post office.

TRICKHAM, TEXAS

WAS ON THE MILITARY ROAD FROM FT. MASON TO FT. BELKNAP IN THE 1850's.

HERE CAMPED JOHNSTON, VAN DORN, LEE, AND OTHER GREAT ARMY MEN.

HERE JOHN CHISUM GATHERED HERDS OF CATTLE IN THE 1860's.

THIS WAS THE LAST TOWN ON THE WESTERN TRAIL TO KANSAS.

COLEMAN COUNTY HISTORICAL COMMITTEE

marker at Trickham

45
stay left on 586
1.5
45
rolling hill country, pasture and low forest
9
573
↗10.5 miles to Mullin
14.2
574
GOLDTHWAITE

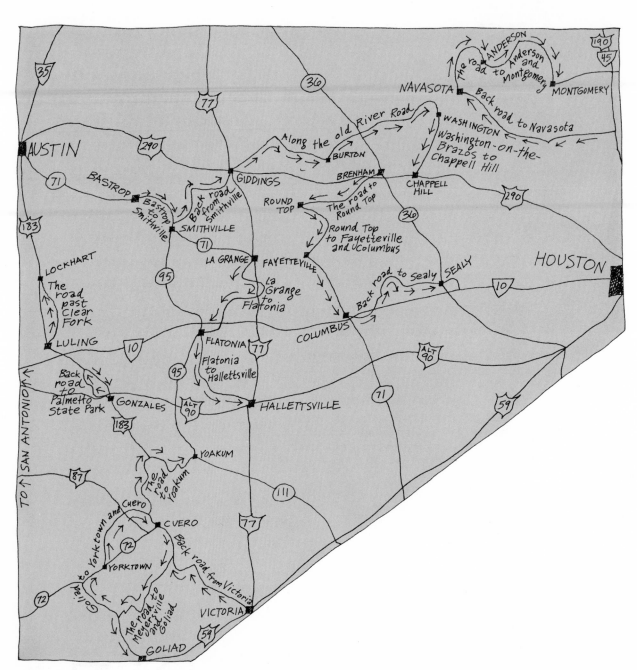

West of Houston
and East
of San Antonio

Rolling, green
hill country encompassed
meadows, forests, and
shaded villages of
infinite charm. Churches,
courthouse squares, and
the Greek Revival and
Victorian architecture
of an earlier time gave
an appealing and
venerable character
to this legendary section
of Texas.

Texas bluebonnet

71

CUERO

183
87
71A

YORKTOWN
17

6.6

236

3157
ARNECKEVILLE

4.6

2.3

Rabel Road
2.8

Albrecht Road

Reineke
Road   1.1

farms
pasture
trees

2.4

447

5.2

Lower Mission Valley Road

1685

1685
swings
left here.
continue
straight
ahead

5.2

236

from
Stayton
and
N. Moody
St. (HWY.
59)

1685 begins
8/10 mile after
crossing river

1685

25 ←
GOLIAD

59

1.9

VICTORIA

Back Road
from Victoria
      I had
wanted to draw
  an armadillo at the Zoological Park
in Victoria, but I learned that their
  only specimen had frozen to death
    during an uncommonly cold winter.
      This delightful zoo specializes
      in showing birds, animals, and other
      creatures native to Texas.

Barn owls of Victoria

The barn owls were remarkably patient, barely moving while I drew them. If I came too close, however, they would lower their heads and bob them at me.

It is well worth exploring Cuero, with its many fine, old homes. You can see them by driving up Terrell Street and down Indianola to Ruess and along Newman on the other side of town.

I sketched a corner of the old Bailey Mills building to represent the early 1900s feeling that pervades the downtown area.

THE BAILEY MILLS BROTHERS 1889

South Main, Cuero

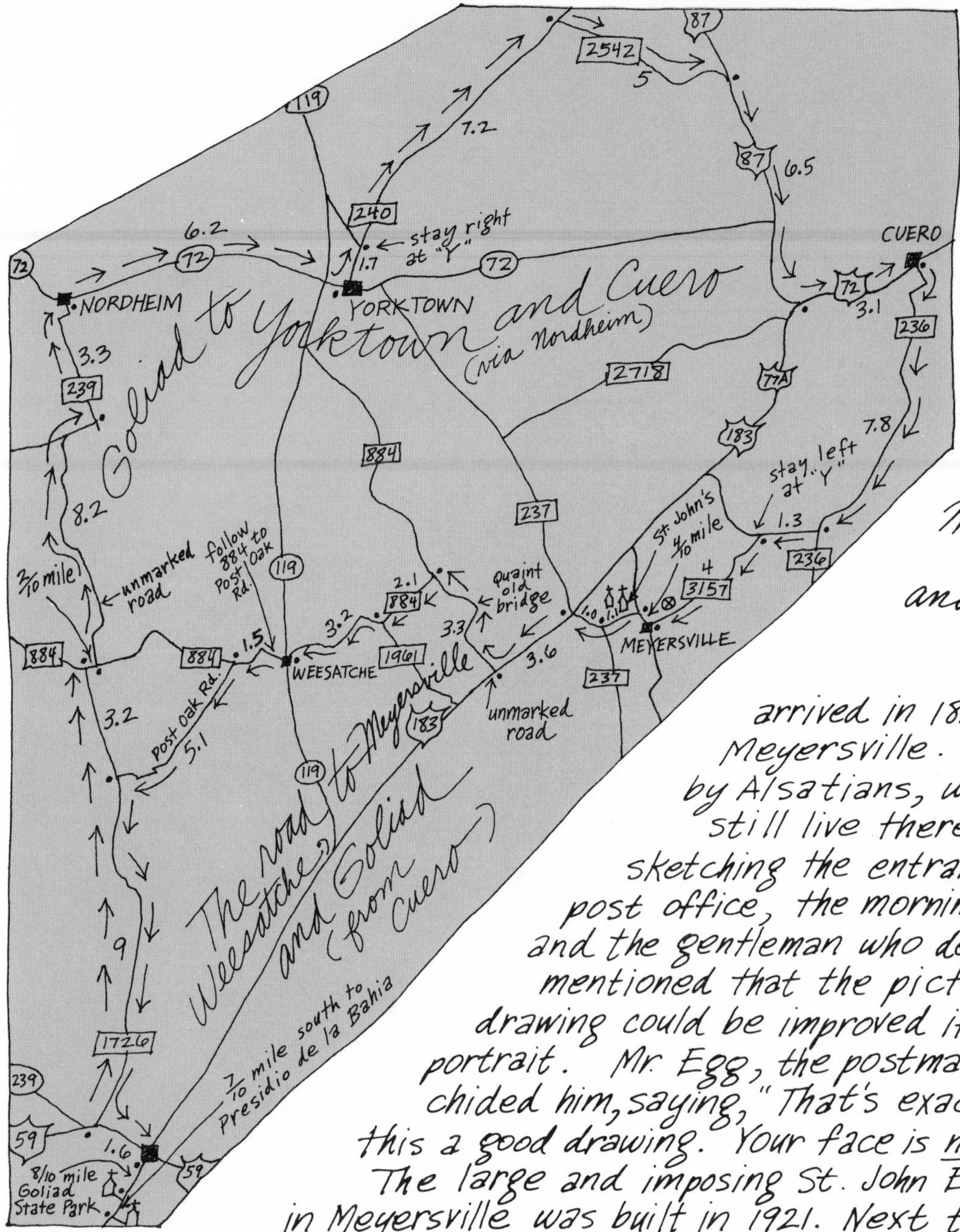

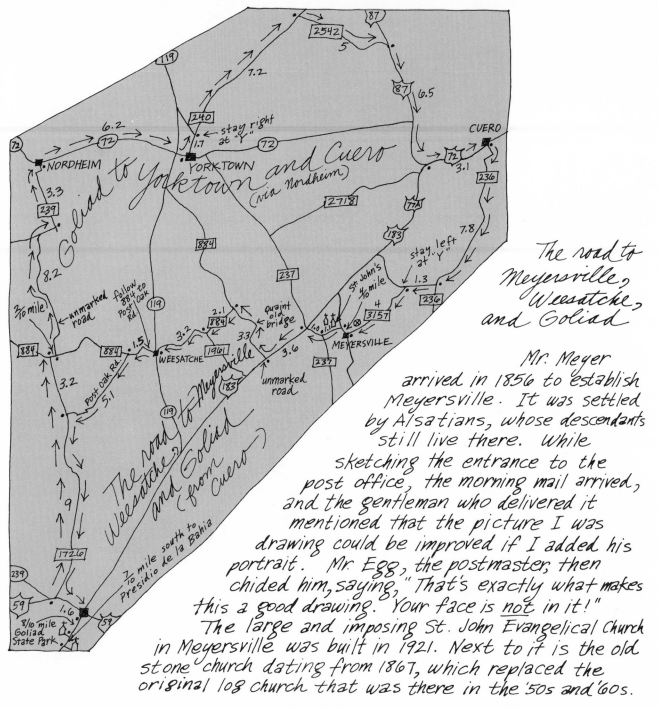

Goliad to Yorktown and Cuero (via Nordheim)
The road to Weesatche, Meyersville and Goliad (from Cuero)
NORDHEIM
YORKTOWN
CUERO
WEESATCHE
MEYERSVILLE
stay right at "Y"
stay left at "Y"
unmarked road
follow 884 to Post Oak Rd.
Post Oak Rd.
quaint old bridge
St. John's 4/10 mile
3/10 mile
unmarked road
7/10 mile south to Presidio de la Bahia
8/10 mile Goliad State Park
72
119
240
2542
87
236
2718
77A
183
884
237
3157
1961
1726
239
59
6.2
1.7
7.2
5
6.5
3.1
3.3
8.2
7.8
1.3
4
2.1
3.2
1.5
3.3
3.6
1.0
1.1
5.1
9
1.6

The road to Meyersville, Weesatche, and Goliad

Mr. Meyer arrived in 1856 to establish Meyersville. It was settled by Alsatians, whose descendants still live there. While sketching the entrance to the post office, the morning mail arrived, and the gentleman who delivered it mentioned that the picture I was drawing could be improved if I added his portrait. Mr. Egg, the postmaster, then chided him, saying, "That's exactly what makes this a good drawing. Your face is <u>not</u> in it!" The large and imposing St. John Evangelical Church in Meyersville was built in 1921. Next to it is the old stone church dating from 1867, which replaced the original log church that was there in the '50s and '60s.

POST OFFICE
MEYERSVILLE, TEX.

Posting a notice
at Meyersville
Post Office

75

Presidio de nuestra Señora
de Loreto de la Bahia

Goliad to Yorktown and Cuero

After looking at the many historic attractions in and around Goliad, including Courthouse Square, Misión Espiritu Santo, and the Fannin Battleground, to name a few, I sketched at the restored Presidio de nuestra Señora de Loreto de la Bahia. It was established in 1749 and is the location where Colonel James Fannin and his troops were executed in 1836 by their Mexican captors during the Texas Revolution. Their burial site at Fannin Memorial is quite near here.

Bluebonnets and Indian paintbrush were the predominant wildflowers along the way to Nordheim. Yorktown was pleasant to visit on the way to Lindenau and Cuero.

HALLETTSVILLE

183

.9

HOCHHEIM
(site)

111

.4

18
77

turn
left on
unmarked
road

2.7

951

1

⁴/₁₀ mile

YOAKUM

½ mile

2.1

1.3

3.1

1

951

13.3

183

766

77

St. John's sketch

1.3

953

2.7

2.4

953

LINDENAU

Road begins
on Heaton St.
(look for E.
Heaton on other
side of street)

1.1

CUERO

2.4

.7

2.6

Tulley Rd.

.6

72,87

72,87
183

78

The road to Hochheim and Yoakum

After the Civil War, the Chisholm trail began here in Cuero, and was used for bringing longhorn cattle to market. It still begins here. Yearly rides memorializing this famous old cattle route begin on this back road out of Cuero. Near Lindenau I drew the St. John's Lutheran Church, with its high wooden tower dominating the landscape.

Only a gas station and a marker identified Hochheim, where in 1856 Valentine Hoch had owned a stage stop. There were many big, beautifully proportioned oaks decorating the road to Yoakum.

St. John's Lutheran Church

Back road bridge
near Gonzales

Back road to Palmetto State Park

The feature of this trip is the picturesque bridge crossing at San Marcos River. Now used only by local traffic, this was once a well-traveled road to San Antonio.

Palmetto State Park, named for the dwarf palmetto, features a botanical garden atmosphere, with some 240 species of birds identified.

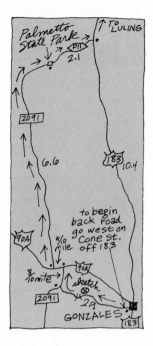

Map 1 labels:
- TO LULING
- Palmetto State Park
- P11
- 2.1
- 2091
- 6.6
- 183 10.4
- to begin back road go west on Cone St. ⁴/₁₀ mile off 183
- 90A
- 90A
- ⅜/₁₀ mile →
- sketch ⊗
- 2091
- 2.9
- GONZALES
- 183

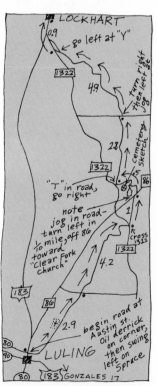

Map 2 labels:
- LOCKHART
- 0.9
- go left at "Y"
- 1322
- 4.9
- turn right then left at jog
- 28
- cemetery sketch
- 1322
- .5 86
- "T" in road, go right
- note jog in road - turn left in ⁴/₁₀ mile, off 86
- 1
- toward "Clear Fork church"
- cross 1322
- 1322
- 4.2
- 183
- 86
- 2.9
- begin road at Austin st. Oil derrick on corner, then swing left on Spruce
- 80
- 90
- LULING
- 80 183 GONZALES 17

The road past Clear Fork

Along the road out of Luling there's many a meadow with cows grazing among pumping jacks. Occasionally the smell of petroleum would assail my nostrils, then fade away as I proceeded.

At a small, tree-shrouded cemetery I sat drawing a headstone with sentimental verse. Birds sang sweetly overhead.

I was impressed by the beauty of the setting.

Headstone at Clear Fork Cemetery

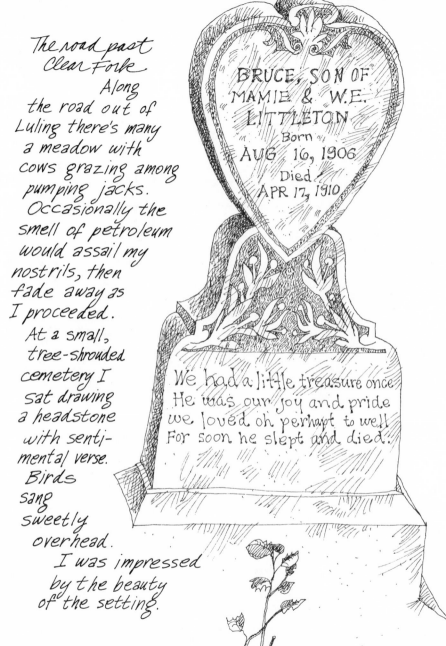

BRUCE, SON OF MAMIE & W.E. LITTLETON
Born AUG 16, 1906
Died APR 17, 1910

We had a little treasure once
He was our joy and pride
We loved oh perhaps to well
For soon he slept and died.

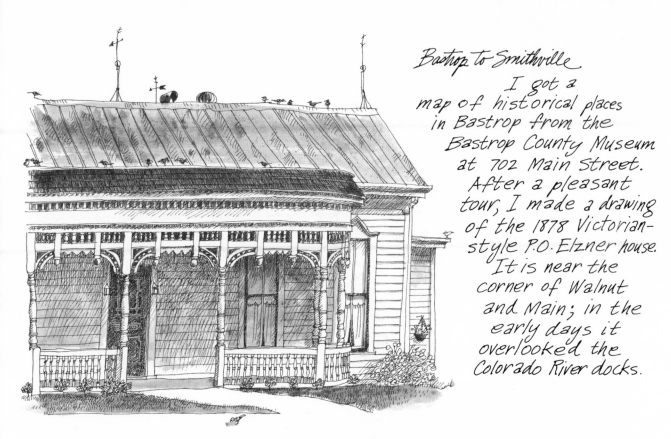

Bastrop to Smithville

I got a map of historical places in Bastrop from the Bastrop County Museum at 702 Main Street. After a pleasant tour, I made a drawing of the 1878 Victorian-style P.O. Elzner house. It is near the corner of Walnut and Main; in the early days it overlooked the Colorado River docks.

Elzner House, Bastrop

At the colorful Bastrop Meat Company, on Main between Chestnut and Pine, I had a hearty lunch of what old-timers here called "hot guts," which, of course, is sausage.

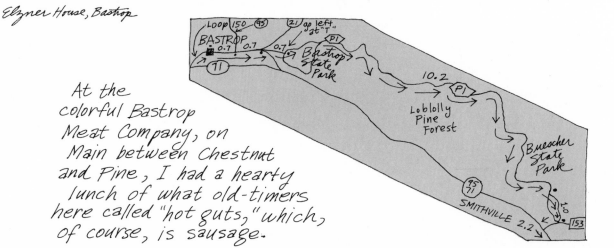

Loop 150 95
BASTROP
0.7 • 0.7 21 go left
at "T"
P1
Bastrop State Park
71 7
10.2
P1
Loblolly Pine Forest
Buescher State Park
95 71
SMITHVILLE 2.2
1.0
153

Even though the average rainfall isn't usually enough to be
expected to support such growth, there were deep
loblolly pine forests along the winding road through
Bastrop and Buescher State Parks.
I roamed the lovely back streets of
Smithville to find an elegant example
of Greek Revival architecture to
draw. Drive out Seventh Street
along the Colorado
River for
other
examples.

On the banks of the Colorado River,
Smithville

Back road from Smithville

Keeping company with the insects,
I sat sketching a landscape of lush, green pasture.
I had to continually pick worms off me that
were dropping from the oak tree above. A large
beetle with coppery-green back circled around
and around the tree. Honeybees buzzed,
grasshoppers fiddled, cows mooed,
and birds twittered.

Along the way to the church of the Wends

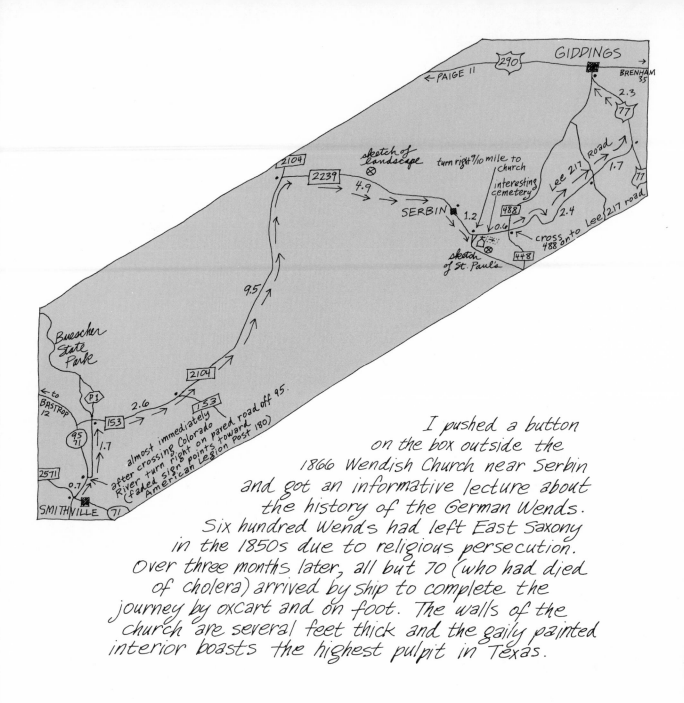

GIDDINGS

290 → BRENHAM 35

← PAIGE 11

2.3

77

2104

2239

4.9

sketch of landscape ⊗

turn right 9/10 mile to church

interesting cemetery

Lee 217

Road

1.7

77

SERBIN 1.2

488

0.6

2.4

cross onto Lee 217 road

cross 488 onto Lee 217 road

⊗

sketch of St. Paul's

448

9.5

Buescher State Park

2104

← to BASTROP 12

P1

2.6

153

153

95 71

almost immediately after crossing Colorado River turn right on paved road off 95. (faded sign points toward American Legion Post 180)

1.7

2571

0.7

SMITHVILLE 71

I pushed a button on the box outside the 1866 Wendish Church near Serbin and got an informative lecture about the history of the German Wends. Six hundred Wends had left East Saxony in the 1850s due to religious persecution. Over three months later, all but 70 (who had died of cholera) arrived by ship to complete the journey by oxcart and on foot. The walls of the church are several feet thick and the gaily painted interior boasts the highest pulpit in Texas.

Saint Paul's
Wendish church

Along the Old River Road

There were views of green forest and farmland, crumbling farmhouses, and vistas of great beauty. I passed a parade of men on horses while going into the little town of Burton, then proceeded toward Gay Hill, passing neat, park-like Gay Hill Farm.

I turned onto a dirt road to see the well-preserved and stately St. Peter Lutheran Church.

At Independence I saw the ruins of old Baylor University (1845-1886) and also visited the town's cypress-shaded cemetery.

Spiderwort

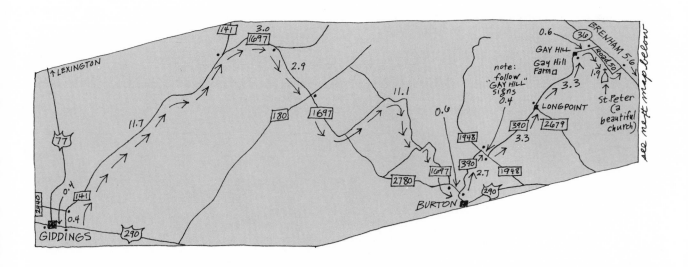

141
3.0
1697
2.9
↑LEXINGTON
11.1
180
1697
0.6
note: follow "GAY HILL" signs
0.4
0.6
BRENHAM 5.6
36
Good 5.0
GAY HILL
Gay Hill Farm□
1.9
St. Peter (a beautiful church)
3.3
■ LONGPOINT
390
2679
11.7
77
3.3
1948
0.4
141
390
2.7
1948
2140
2780
1697
BURTON
290
0.4
GIDDINGS
290

see next map below

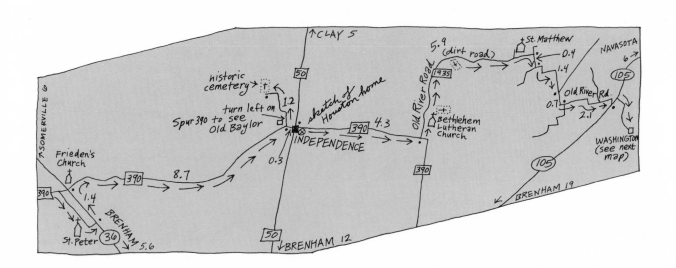

↑CLAY 5
5.9 (dirt road)
✝ St. Matthew
0.4
NAVASOTA
6
50
1.4
105
historic cemetery → ✝
1935
1.2
turn left on Spur 390 to see Old Baylor
sketch of Houston home
Old River Road
0.7
Old River Rd.
SOMERVILLE ○
390
4.3
2.1
INDEPENDENCE
✝ Bethlehem Lutheran Church
WASHINGTON (see next map)
Frieden's Church
0.3
390
8.7
390
390
105
1.4
BRENHAM 19
390
BRENHAM 5.6
St. Peter
36
5.6
50
↓BRENHAM 12

89

I sketched Martha Lea Houston's house in Independence. She was General Sam Houston's widow and lived there with her eight children from 1863 to 1867.

Martha Houston House

Washington-on-the-Brazos to Chappell Hill

Colonel William Fairfax Gray visited Washington-on-the-Brazos in 1836 as a representative of a land-buying firm from Washington, D.C. Portions of his diary are on exhibit at the Star of the Republic Museum, Washington-on-the-Brazos State Park. One notation, made on Saturday, February 27, 1836, must have inspired me to draw the kitchen table composition on the following page. "The wind yesterday blew hard from the north right in my face; a most uncomfortable ride. Left Edwards after breakfast; stopt at Mrs. Panky's to feed my horse where I got an excellent dinner of bacon, turnip tops, boiled eggs, coffee and milk, with fine cornbread. I relished it more than any meal I have eaten in Texas. Dinner and room fifty-six cents."

Be sure to see the United Methodist Church of Chappell Hill, at Church and Poplar Streets. Its colorful stained glass windows accent the cheerful, white exterior and are glorious to view inside.

Kitchen table at Washington-on-the-Brazos

The road to Round Top

             There were many old Texan homes here, and additional ones have been transplanted from other areas to give Round Top a charming, antiquated look. Settler Trangott Wandke's cabinet shop is featured in my picture. He was a skilled worker in wood, having constructed a cedar pipe organ for the Round Top Bethlehem Church, pictured here also.

Nearby is
Festival Hill, where major
musical events are held in summer.
Four miles east of Round Top is
Winedale Historical Center, with
restored nineteenth century
plantation homes, log cabins,
a smokehouse, and barns on
exhibit by the University of
Texas at Austin.

Back street in
Round Top

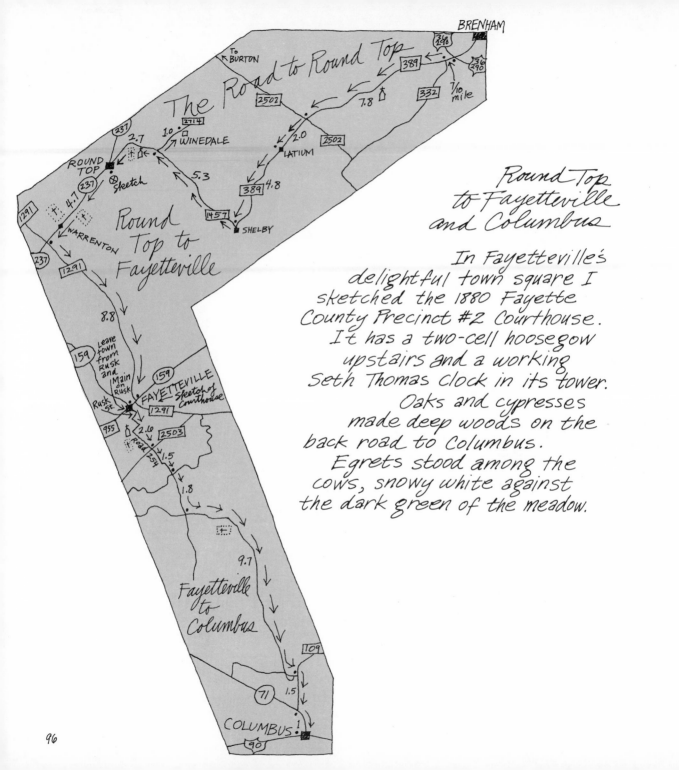

The Road to Round Top

BRENHAM

To BURTON

389

332

7/10 mile

36 290

2502

7.8

2502

2714

2.0

LATIUM

2.7

10.

WINEDALE

389

4.8

237

ROUND TOP

5.3

237

Sketch

1457

SHELBY

1291

4.7

WARRENTON

Round Top to Fayetteville

237

1291

8.8

159

Leave town from Rusk and Main on Rusk

159

FAYETTEVILLE

Sketch of Courthouse

Rusk St.

1291

955

2.6

2503

Road 254

1.5

1.8

9.7

Fayetteville to Columbus

109

71

1.5

COLUMBUS

1

90

Round Top
to Fayetteville
and Columbus

In Fayetteville's
delightful town square I
sketched the 1880 Fayette
County Precinct #2 Courthouse.
It has a two-cell hoosegow
upstairs and a working
Seth Thomas clock in its tower.
Oaks and cypresses
made deep woods on the
back road to Columbus.
Egrets stood among the
cows, snowy white against
the dark green of the meadow.

Courthouse in
the square,
Fayetteville

Columbus is a
town of massive live oaks.
Some grow in the streets,
and their low branches deny
passage to large vehicles.

Columbus, town of oaks

LA GRANGE

77

159

71

71

Monument Hill State Park

1.6

155

77

9.4

4.6

1383

AMMANNSVILLE

1965

2.9

1383

155

2.2

3171

sketch of church

956

1.5

0.9

1.2

956

FREYBURG

2238

1.5

well kept cemetery

Freyburg Church

old store

0.6

2672

77

0.5

1.6

turn left on Road 448, then in ½ mile, go right on dirt road

Freyburg Community Hall and Gemütlichkeit Beer Garden

2238

3.1

10

0.9

FLATONIA

90

6/10 mile

12-95

3.4

PRAHA

Freyburg Church on the horizon

La Grange to Praha

La Grange was located where an old Indian trail crossed the Colorado River. It became the seat of Fayette County in 1837.

Leaving the shaded streets of this history-filled town, I stopped first at Monument Hill State Park, grave site for Texas soldiers who died for the preservation of the republic. Then I traveled south across the broad farmland toward Flatonia stopping in Praha.

Near Freyburg I sat under a tree in the local cemetery to draw a view of the United Methodist Church in its rural setting.

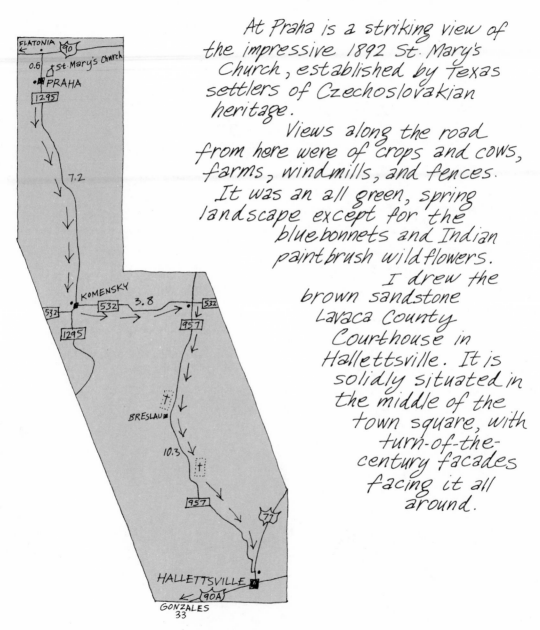

Praha to Hallettsville

At Praha is a striking view of the impressive 1892 St. Mary's Church, established by Texas settlers of Czechoslovakian heritage.

Views along the road from here were of crops and cows, farms, windmills, and fences. It was an all green, spring landscape except for the bluebonnets and Indian paintbrush wildflowers.

I drew the brown sandstone Lavaca County Courthouse in Hallettsville. It is solidly situated in the middle of the town square, with turn-of-the-century facades facing it all around.

Lavaca County Courthouse, Hallettsville

103

Back road to Sealy

Surrounded by roaring trucks on Interstate 10, I hastened onto Alleyton Road out of Columbus. Alleyton was a key point on the supply line of the Confederate states during the Civil War and a main destination of wagon trains returning from the Rio Grande.

Along Mentz Road I sketched a stately Greek-Revival-style mansion. The drive had been through attractive countryside and forest, ending near Sealy at Stephen F. Austin State Park, where statues, monuments, an old store, and a "dog-run" cabin were on display.

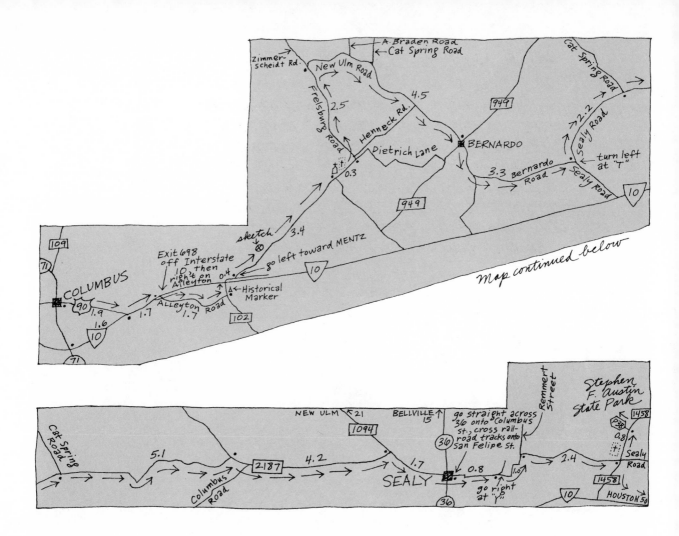

A. Braden Road
← Cat Spring Road

Zimmer-
scheidt Rd.

New Ulm Road

Cat Spring Road

Freisburg Road

2.5

4.5

949

2.2

Sealy Road

Henneck Rd.

Dietrich Lane

BERNARDO

turn left at "T"

0.3

3.3 Bernardo Road → Sealy Road

10

949

109

71

sketch

3.4

go left toward MENTZ

Map continued below

Exit 698 off Interstate 10, then right on Alleyton

COLUMBUS

0.4

10

90

1.9

1.6

1.7

Alleyton Road

1.7

Historical Marker

102

71

10

71

Cat Spring Road

5.1

2-187

4.2

Columbus Road

NEW ULM 21

1094

BELLVILLE 15

go straight across 36 onto Columbus St., cross railroad tracks onto San Felipe St.

Remmert Street

Stephen F. Austin State Park

1458

36

0.8

2.4

Sealy Road

1.7

SEALY

0.8

1.0

1458

36

go right at "Y"

10

HOUSTON 50

along the road to Mentz

105

Back road to Navasota

There were a number of picture-worthy churches in the country town of Navasota. St. Paul's Episcopal Church at McAlpine and Cannon Streets, the one I selected to draw, was designed by architect Ernest Lord in 1891. It is a replica of St. Michael's in Coventry, England, a cathedral that Mr. Lord had attended.

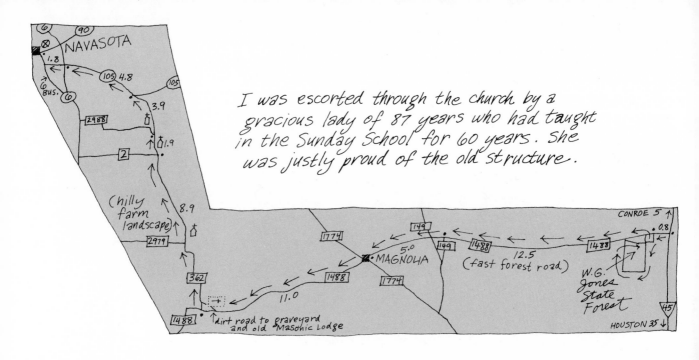

I was escorted through the church by a gracious lady of 87 years who had taught in the Sunday School for 60 years. She was justly proud of the old structure.

There is a statue in Navasota to the memory of the early explorer and colonizer Robert Cavelier Sieur de la Salle. One hundred thirty years before this Anglo-American settlement in Texas had begun, la Salle landed his fleet of three ships at Matagorda Bay to begin a coastal colony called Fort St. Louis.

Unfortunately, he was murdered by one of his men some two years later while exploring near the present town of Navasota.

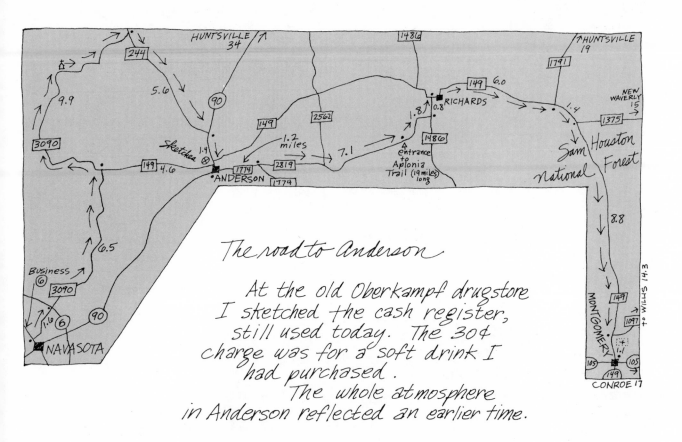

HUNTSVILLE 34

244

5.6

90

9.9

3090

149 4.6

Sketched 1.4

ANDERSON

1774

1774

2562

149

1.2 miles

2819

7.1

entrance to Aplonia Trail (19 miles long)

1486

1486

1.8

0.8 RICHARDS

149 6.0

1.4

1791

↑HUNTSVILLE 19

NEW WAVERLY 15

1375

Sam Houston National Forest

8.8

149

MONTGOMERY

1097

1.1

105

149

105

CONROE 17

to WILLIS 14.3

6.5

Business 6

3090

1.6 6

90

NAVASOTA

The road to Anderson

At the old Oberkampf drugstore I sketched the cash register, still used today. The 30¢ charge was for a soft drink I had purchased.
The whole atmosphere in Anderson reflected an earlier time.

108

In the drug store
at Anderson

At the end of the main street sits the 1891 Grimes County Courthouse. A Clyde Barrow gang member who was on trial here in the 1930s vowed he'd see the court in infernal regions.

anderson

Anderson is so small that people can shout a conversation from one end of town to the other, and while I made my drawing, some did.

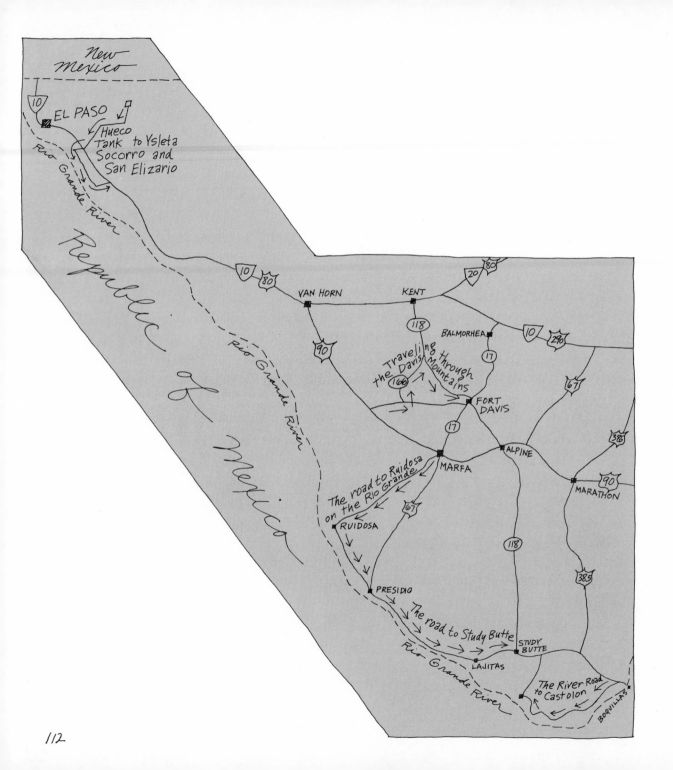

New Mexico

10

EL PASO

Hueco Tank to Ysleta Socorro and San Elizario

Rio Grande River

Republic of Mexico

Rio Grande River

10 80

VAN HORN

KENT

20 80

118

BALMORHEA

10 290

17

90

Traveling Through the Davis Mountains

166

67

FORT DAVIS

17

38

MARFA

ALPINE

The road to Ruidosa on the Rio Grande

90

MARATHON

67

RUIDOSA

118

PRESIDIO

38.5

The road to Study Butte

STUDY BUTTE

LAJITAS

Rio Grande River

The River Road to Castolon

BOQUILLAS

Southwest Texas and the Big Bend Country

Here are mountains of Texas lifting six, seven, and eight thousand feet to the heavens. Some of these are the mountains that created the big bend in the course of the Rio Grande.

The best back roads in this part of Texas, for me, seemed to follow or seek the great river.

A sense of wonder and curiosity filled me to stand along the Rio Grande in a lonely spot and gaze across at neighboring Mexico.

Evening Primrose
(Buttercup)

Hueco Tanks to Ysleta, Socorro, and San Elizario
Hueco Tanks has an interesting collection of canyons to hike. The natural limestone cisterns there gather and hold water; thus the name Hueco, or "hollow." The tanks were a regular watering stop in 1859 for Butterfield overland mail riders. Pictographs attest to their use by the earliest Indian travelers.

Boulders at Hueco Tanks

114

At Hueco Tanks I sketched big boulders balanced and wedged together. I also noted some pictographs and added them to the picture. While I was drawing, shouts and laughter of a troup of El Paso Boy Scouts greeted my ears, and a desert bird flew into the rocky interior warbling a crisp and lovely musical scale.

The site of the first Spanish mission in Texas in 1682 was at Ysleta. At Misión Nuestra Señora del Carmen, I made a drawing of the cast bronze bell that is in front of the church.

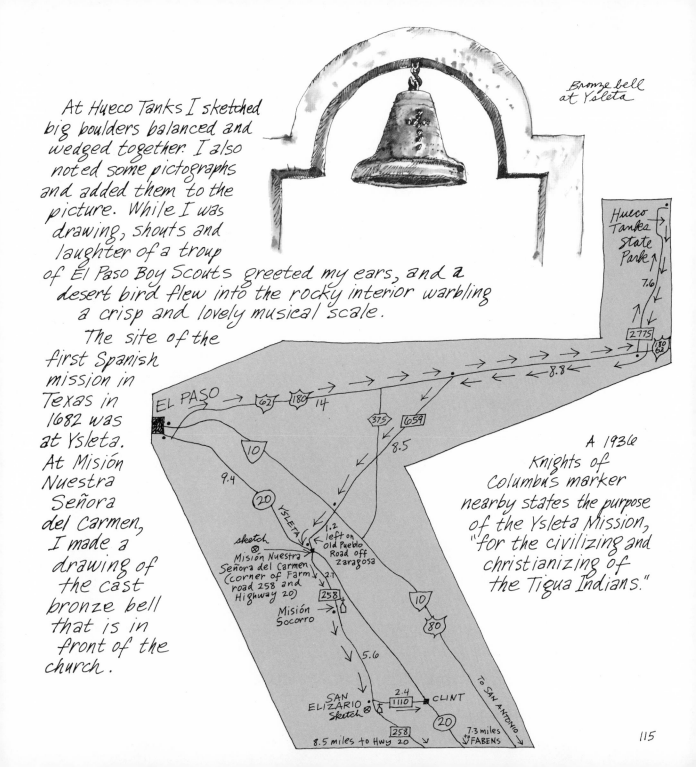

Bronze bell at Ysleta

A 1936 Knights of Columbus marker nearby states the purpose of the Ysleta Mission, "for the civilizing and christianizing of the Tigua Indians."

Hueco Tanks State Park

7.6

2.775

8.8

EL PASO

62 180 14

375 659

8.5

10

9.4

20

YSLETA

sketch ⊗
Misión Nuestra Señora del Carmen (corner of Farm road 258 and Highway 20)

1.2 left on Old Pueblo Road off Zaragosa

2.7

258

Misión Socorro

10

80

5.6

SAN ELIZARIO Sketch ⊗

2.4
1110

CLINT

20

To SAN ANTONIO

7.3 miles to FABENS

258

8.5 miles to Hwy 20

115

At San Elizario
I sat in the entrance
to the local police
department to sketch
the square. Gaily
chirping swallows
flew in erratic patterns
to and from nests above
my head. To my right
was the San Elizario
Presidio Chapel, and in the
square was a bright blue-green
gazebo shaded by
cottonwood trees.

San Elizario

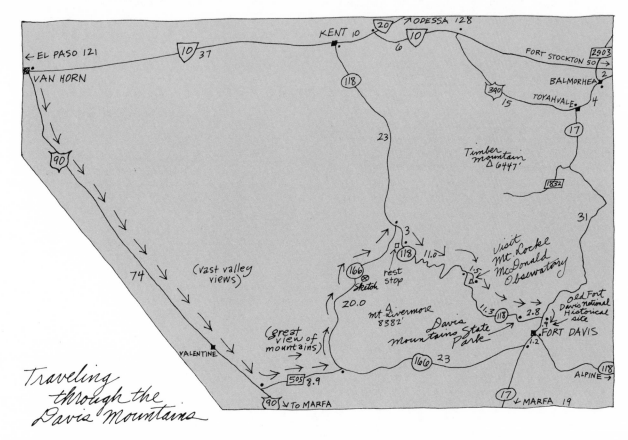

← EL PASO 121 | 10 37 | KENT 10 | 20 | ODESSA 128 | FORT STOCKTON 50 → | 2903

VAN HORN

10

6

10

118

BALMORHEA | 2

TOYAHVALE | 4

340 15

90

23

17

Timber mountain △ 6447'

1832

74

(vast valley views)

31

3

118 11.0

Visit Mt. Locke McDonald Observatory

166 ⊗ *Sketch*

rest stop

1.2

20.0

1.3 118 2.8

Old Fort Davis national Historical site

mt. Livermore △ 8382'

Davis Mountains State Park

FORT DAVIS

1.2

VALENTINE

(great view of mountains)

166 23

118

ALPINE →

505 8.9

90 ↓ TO MARFA

17 ↓ MARFA 19

Traveling through the Davis Mountains

This was high country. McDonald Observatory, with its 107 inch telescope, is at about 6800 feet. Pinyon pines grow here and juniper textures the mountain sides. The air was clear and crisply cool.

I sketched one of the salmon-colored, rocky mountains along the way and was pleased to sight a herd of pronghorn antelope.

driving through the Davis Mountains

Old Fort Davis

Fort Davis, as I sketched it in its volcanic rock setting, faced directly toward the rising sun. This west Texas outpost was created to guard immigrants, freighters, and stagecoaches against hostile raids by Comanche and Apache Indians on the old San Antonio-El Paso road. The first, more primitive fort was established in 1854. The second fort was used until 1891. Although at present much of Fort Davis has disappeared, there was a significant portion of it still there that was most fascinating to see.

The road to Ruidosa on the Rio Grande

There was significant mountain scenery along this little-used back road, especially of lofty Chinati Peak, 7730 feet high. Farmland views changed to hillsides of blooming yucca.

Later I forded streams bordered with cottonwoods. A jackrabbit, the sun accenting his long pink ears, bounded along the road not knowing which way to turn to escape my vehicle.

At the quiet village of Ruidosa I could hear chickens crowing from the state of Chihuahua across the Rio Grande.

With La Frontera bar to my left, I sketched two relaxed goats chewing their cud on the steps of a decaying adobe church.

MARFA
17
90
The Road to Ruidosa
32
2810
67
169
dirt road begins
Dead end
sketch
19.5
RUIDOSA
(grand scenery)
170
Chinati Peak 7730'
Rio Grande River
21.2
colorful cemeteries
Republic
5.3
rest stop
10.7
PRESIDIO
3.5
visit Fort Leaton Historic Site
170
Rio Grande River
The road to Study Butte
of
Mexico
33.0
Rio Grande River
rest area
sketch of Rio Grande
2.76
12.5
170
LAJITAS
ALPINE 72
118
sketch of dwelling
TERLINGUA
4.5
STUDY BUTTE
118
PANTHER JUNCTION 10

goats of Ruidosa

123

The road to Study Butte

With outspread wings, a black vulture posed on a post alongside the road to catch the sun's early morning rays.

A coyote trotted through waist-high desert bluebonnets and spindly ocotillo.

There were views of the Chihuahua mountains and villages on the Mexican side of the Rio Grande. I sketched the river where it made a turn past an orange and pink rocky prominence. A rubber raft slid through some rapids while children shouted gleefully.

The Rio Grande near Lajitas

At the site of the bygone 248 mine near Terlingua I sketched a thick-walled rock dwelling. This is desert country, and I sat in the doorway of another rock hut to be sheltered from the hot sun. My diversion while there was the drama of a huge black bee guarding the entrance from the intrusion of a certain yellow wasp. They buzzed and hummed at one another for the entire time I was there, with the black bee always successfully chasing the wasp away.

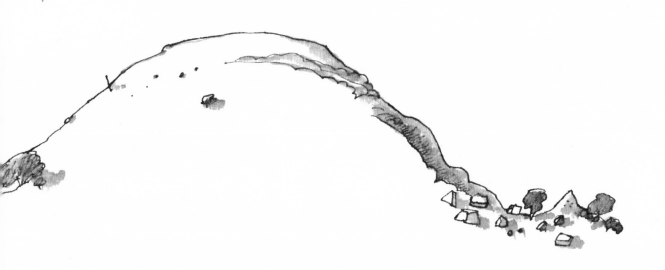

Dwelling at the old
248 mine near Terlingua

↑ALPINE 77

118

13

↑MARATHON 69

PANTHER JUNCTION

TERLINGUA (site) 170

118 STUDY BUTTE 11

⊗ sketch of Chisos Mountains

Park Headquarters

Note: Check Park Headquarters for latest River Road conditions. Detailed Map of Big Bend National Park available at low cost.

Chisos Mountains

21

20.6

see Boquillas Canyon and border crossing

River Road begins here (dirt road)

← 3.2 ←

1.1 RIO GRANDE VILLAGE

Gravel Pit Road 1.8

3.5 →

Old San Vicente Road 1.6

Picnic grounds

Cottonwood Campground

1.9

Casa de Piedra Road 2.5

BOQUILLAS

Glenn Springs Road

River Road ends here (I measured the trip at 50.6 miles)

0.9 1.2

unmarked road

CASTOLON

10.3

Black Dike Road

Sierra Chino Road

Guaging Station Road

Dominguez Spring Trail (about 6 miles)

Views of Chisos Mountains

roughest section of road

2.3 ⊗ sketch of Mariscal mine

5.2

.1

Rooney's Road

Republic of Mexico

Republic of Mexico

2.2

1.3 2.2

1.4 2.5

6.0

4.1

2.2

Solis Road

Talley Road

(View of river)

128

Big Bend National Park's River Road

Along this road there are many views of the richly-patterned Chisos (Ghost) Mountains of Big Bend National Park.

Miners who once worked the now-deserted Mariscal mine transported cinnabar to Terlingua by mule. From a distance the old mine resembled a haunted Indian village.

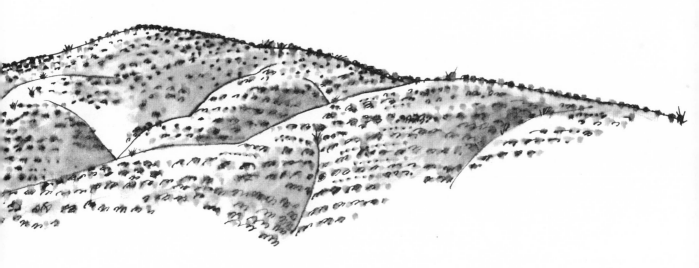

Mariscal mine seen from River Road

The Chisos Mountains,
Big Bend National Park

130

131

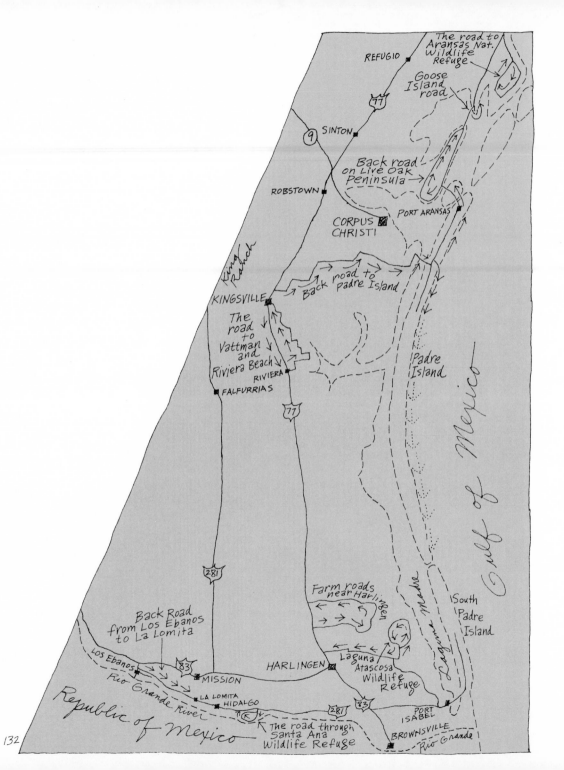

The road to
Aransas Nat.
Wildlife
Refuge

REFUGIO

Goose
Island
road

77

SINTON

9

Back road
on Live Oak
Peninsula

ROBSTOWN

PORT ARANSAS

CORPUS
CHRISTI

King Ranch

Back road to Padre Island

KINGSVILLE

The
road
to
Vattman
and
Riviera Beach

Padre
Island

RIVIERA

FALFURRIAS

77

281

Gulf of Mexico

Farm roads
near Harlingen

South
Padre
Island

Back Road
from Los Ebanos
to La Lomita

Laguna Madre

LOS EBANOS

83

MISSION

HARLINGEN

Laguna
Atascosa
Wildlife
Refuge

Rio Grande River

LA LOMITA
HIDALGO

281

83

PORT
ISABEL

Republic of Mexico

The road through
Santa Ana
Wildlife Refuge

BROWNSVILLE

Rio Grande

132

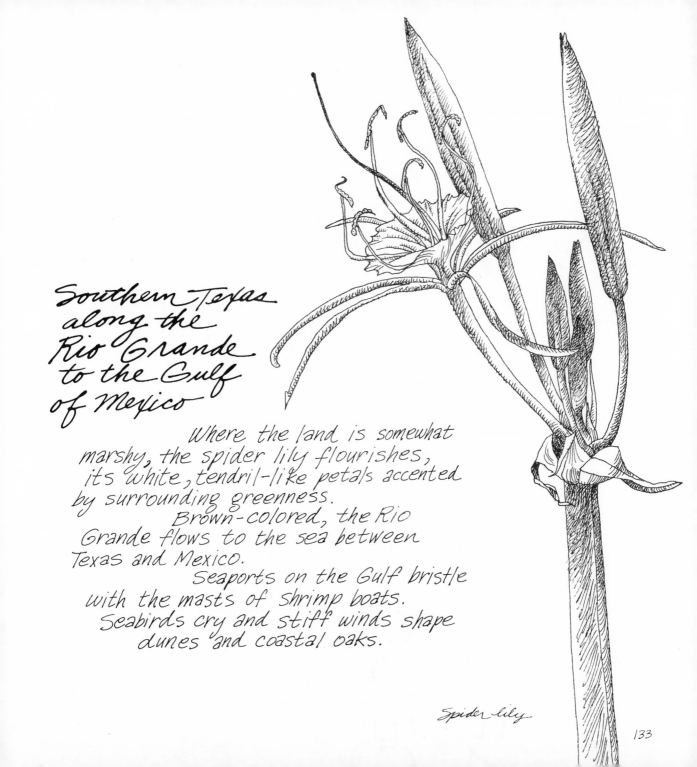

Southern Texas
along the
Rio Grande
to the Gulf
of Mexico

Where the land is somewhat
marshy, the spider lily flourishes,
its white, tendril-like petals accented
by surrounding greenness.
Brown-colored, the Rio
Grande flows to the sea between
Texas and Mexico.
Seaports on the Gulf bristle
with the masts of shrimp boats.
Seabirds cry and stiff winds shape
dunes and coastal oaks.

Spider lily

134

Back road from Los Ebanos to La Lomita

The ancient ford at Los Ebanos (The Ebonies) was first noted by José de Escandon in the 1740s. The day I sketched this scene, a hand-pulled ferry carried autos across the Rio Grande for 75¢, passengers for 10¢. One end of the ferry cable is strung to a massive ebony tree on the Texas side. The traffic was made up of local people going to or from Los Ebanos and the village of Gustavo Diaz Ordaz, a mile south on the Mexican side. When there was a lull in the ferrying, the boat operators would come to see how my drawing was progressing.

Hand-pulled ferry on the Rio Grande

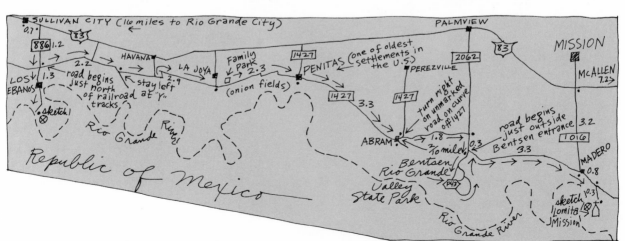

SULLIVAN CITY (16 miles to Rio Grande City)
0.7
886 1.2
83
HAVANA
2.2
road begins
just north
of railroad at "y"
tracks
LA JOYA
stay left
2.9
LOS
EBANOS
1.3
sketch
Rio Grande River
Republic of Mexico
Family
Park
2.3
(onion fields)
PENITAS (one of oldest
settlements in
the U.S.)
1427
1427
3.3
ABRAM
1.8
7/10 miles
Bentsen
Rio Grande
Valley
State Park
243
Rio Grande River
PALMVIEW
83
MISSION
2062
PEREZVILLE
McALLEN
7.2
1427
turn right
on unmarked
road on curve
off 1427
0.3
road begins
just outside
Bentsen entrance 3.2
3.3
1016
MADERO
0.8
sketch 0.3
Lomita
Mission

Capilla de la Lomita

I drove through
miles of farmland,
arriving finally at the
Capilla de la Lomita, "Chapel
of the Little Hill." The nearby
town of Mission was named
in honor of this old landmark.
It was a simple building
and, in its setting,
a place inspiring
contemplation.

137

Path along the Rio Grande
with Chachalaca

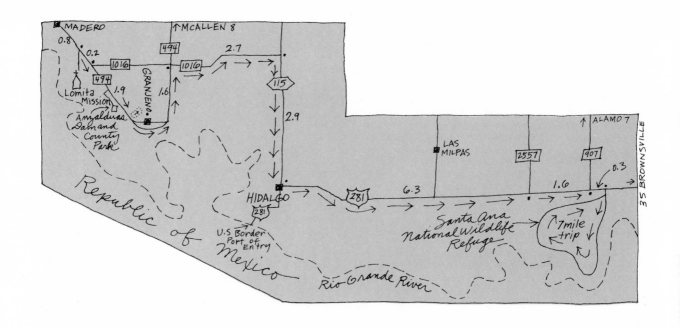

The road through Santa Ana Wildlife Refuge

     Along the Rio Grande, where agriculture has largely taken over all the land, this sanctuary of nature is the largest piece of natural vegetation left. Trees preserved here are the elm, ebony, hackberry, ash, anaqua, tepeguaje, guayacan, huisache, and others. Birds include: the kiskadee flycatcher, white-collared seedeater, chachalaca, and red-billed pigeon. A sign by the side of the road through the refuge warned, "Drive slowly, chachalacas in the road." Early morning or late afternoon are said to be the best times to observe wildlife.

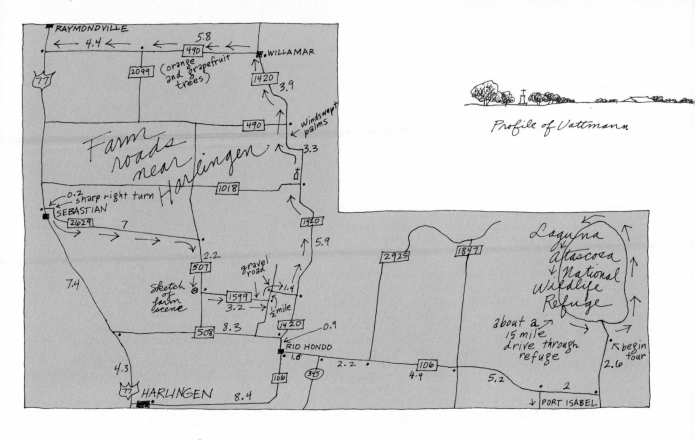

RAYMONDVILLE

← 4.4 ← ← 5.8 ←

490

[77] 2099 (orange and grapefruit trees) [WILLAMAR]

1420

3.9

Farm roads near Harlingen

490 ← Windswept palms

3.3

1018

← 0.2 sharp right turn

SEBASTIAN

2629 7 →

2.2

507

gravel road

Sketch of farm scene → 1599 ← 1.4

3.2 → ½ mile

508 8.3 1420

0.9

RIO HONDO

1.6

106 345 2.2 106

4.4

7.4

4.3

[77] HARLINGEN 8.4

1420

5.9

2925 1847

Laguna Atascosa National Wildlife Refuge

about a 15 mile drive through refuge

↳ begin tour

2.6

5.2 2

↓ PORT ISABEL

Profile of Vattmann

Farm scene near Harlingen

Farm roads near Harlingen

Long rows of planted fields stretched to a horizon straight as a ruler. Heavy grey clouds threatened rain, the sun occasionally breaking through to light a portion of the vast farmland.

Laguna Atascosa National Wildlife Refuge

The Bayside Tour, fifteen miles long, takes you through the southernmost waterfowl refuge in the "Central Flyway," which extends from Canada to the Gulf. It is a wintering area for ducks and geese and part of our national effort to preserve, manage, and protect wildlife populations and habitats.

The road to Vattmann and Riviera Beach

There was a striking, pink brick church at Vattmann. German settlers had been encouraged by the King ranch to farm and live there. They prospered and built this large church.

Loyola and Riviera Beach on the Cayo del Grullo were colorful fishing villages to visit.

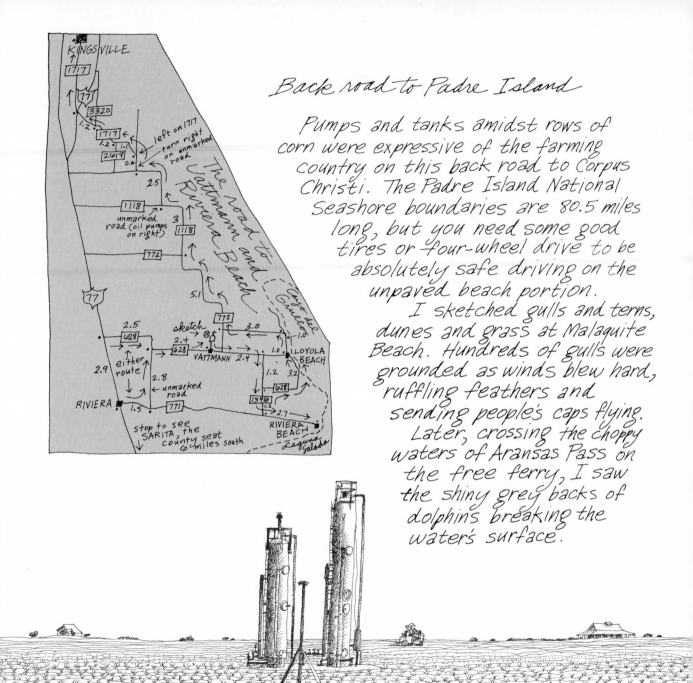

Back road to Padre Island

Pumps and tanks amidst rows of corn were expressive of the farming country on this back road to Corpus Christi. The Padre Island National Seashore boundaries are 80.5 miles long, but you need some good tires or four-wheel drive to be absolutely safe driving on the unpaved beach portion.

I sketched gulls and terns, dunes and grass at Malaquite Beach. Hundreds of gulls were grounded as winds blew hard, ruffling feathers and sending people's caps flying.

Later, crossing the choppy waters of Aransas Pass on the free ferry, I saw the shiny grey backs of dolphins breaking the water's surface.

Map labels:

KINGSVILLE
1717
77
3320
1.2
1717
1.2 · 1.1
2619
0.6
left on 1717 — turn right on unmarked road
2.5
1118
unmarked road (oil pumps on right)
3
1118
772
77
5.1
The road to Vattmann and Riviera Beach (Cayo del Grullo)
2.5
628
sketch
772
3.0
2.4
628
VATTMANN 2.4
1.0
LOYOLA BEACH
2.9
either route
2.8
← unmarked road
RIVIERA
1.5
771
1.2 3.2
1.0
628
1596
1.2 2.7
RIVIERA BEACH
Laguna Salada
stop to see SARITA, the county seat 6 miles south

Tanks amidst the corn

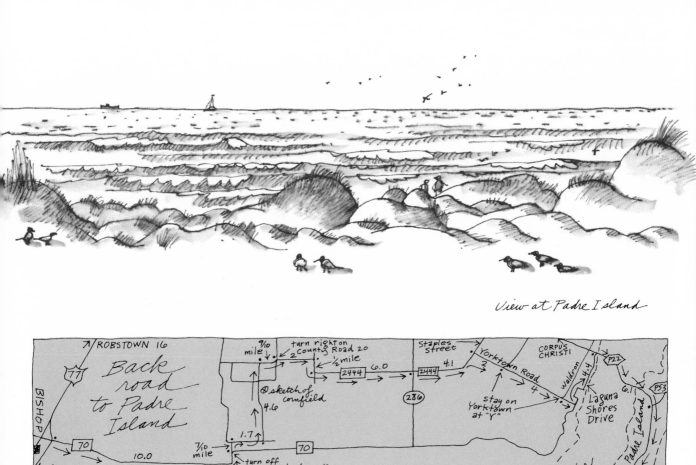

View at Padre Island

Back road to Padre Island

ROBSTOWN 16

77

BISHOP

77

KINGSVILLE 6

70

10.0

7/10 mile

1.7

turn off 70 (unmarked road)

70

4.6

7/10 mile

2

⊗ sketch of cornfield

turn right on County Road 20

½ mile

2444

6.0

2444

286

4.1

Staples Street

Yorktown Road

2

stay on Yorktown at "Y"

4

CORPUS CHRISTI

Waldron

Yorktown Road

4.4

P22

6.1

P53

Laguna Shores Drive

Padre Island

P22

11.7

Laguna Madre

Gulf of Mexico

entry point of Padre Island National Seashore

5.5

Ranger Station

⊗ Malaquite Beach

for 4-wheel drive travel

Padre Island

Back road on Live Oak Peninsula

Aransas Pass is a shrimp boat town. The fleet—big, rugged looking craft, black nets aloft—look a powerful adversary for the little pink shrimp. Newly painted white and bright orange the boat I sketched seemed ready for sea.

Aransas Pass shrimp boat

145

Goose
Island
Road

Copano
Bay

35

2.8 ⊗ sketch

Goose Island State Park

P13

35 2.6

cross 35 to
Fulton Beach
Road (no sign)

6.3

35 ⊗ sketch of
oak trees

↓4.4

1781

3036 FULTON
historic
Fulton
home

2.6

1781 2165

Aransas Bay

↑ROCKPORT

5.3 881

881 Oak Peninsula

881

1069

Back road on Live

4.2

Travel these
roads to see
fishing
fleet

35

sketch of
shrimp boat

ARANSAS
PASS

⊗ Stapp Street
Bigelow Street
Huff Street
Wilson Ave

3.6 35

1069

Commercial
Street 2

361

361

To Mustang Island

7 miles to Port Aransas

361

INGLESIDE

1069

4.9

Ingleside
Cove

1069

INGLESIDE-
ON-THE-BAY
(a pleasant village)

2725

3.4

Redfish Bay

Windswept oaks near Fulton

Goose Island road

Signs showed me the way
to Texas's "champion" live
oak. Over 1000 years old,
it was already a giant
when Cabeza de Vaca and
Sieur de la Salle explored the
coast in the 1500s and 1600s.
It is still a healthy
looking, colossal old oak.

Pink evening primrose

Goose Island oak

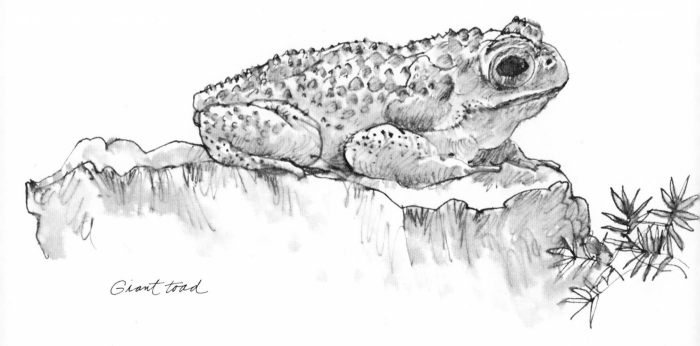

Giant toad

The road to Aransas National
Wildlife Refuge
        The whooping
crane has a home here, arriving
in October and November and
staying until early April. And
this is where Jean Lafitte, the
pirate, is said to have disbanded
his crew and buried his treasure.
     The 55,000 acre refuge
protects the disappearing
wildlife of coastal Texas.
    There are many, many
birds other than the cranes,
as well as wildlife of
all variety, including
deer, alligators and
giant toads.

35 TO PORT LA VACA 21

Hynes Bay

239
5.6

AUSTWELL

3035

1684

1684 2 774

2040

7.1

774

774

35

6.4

Aransas
Wildlife
Refuge
entrance
(about a 17
mile round
trip from
this point)

San Antonio Bay

13.6

Aransas
Wildlife   National
            Refuge

ayres
Bay

Mesquite
Bay

St. Charles Bay

Goose
Island
State
Park

Carlos Bay

35 ↙ ARANSAS PASS

151

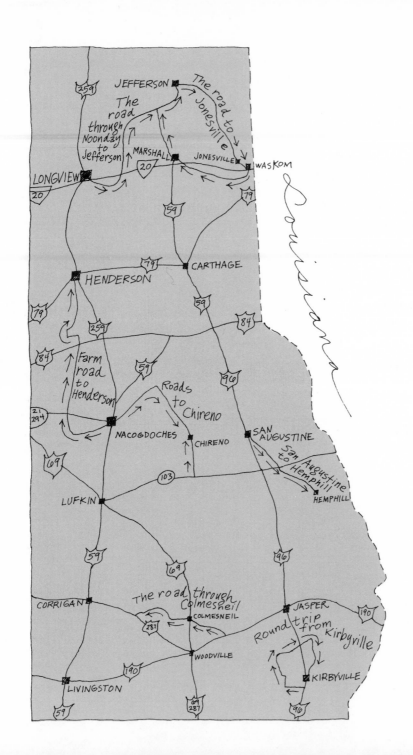

152

Northeast Texas

Meadows, forest, green rolling hills, wildflowers, bayous, farms, and streams inspire the nature seeker along the tranquil back roads of northeastern Texas.

Rain lily

Sharecropper's cabin near Roganville

Round trip from Kirbyville

This road passed the former location of a town called Pinetucky. It was abandoned when the railroad was built through nearby Kirbyville. Pinetucky has become forest again.

It was raining as I sketched this old sharecropper's cabin in the forest.

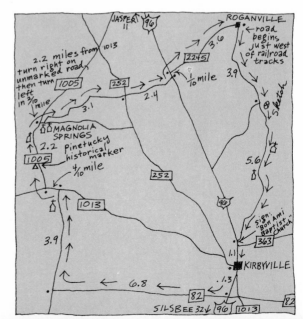

JASPER 11 | 96
1013
ROGANVILLE
road begins just west of railroad tracks
2.2 miles from turn right on unmarked road then turn left in 3/10 mile
1005
252
2245
1/10 mile
3.6
3.9
3.1
2.4
Sketch
MAGNOLIA SPRINGS
2.2 Pinetucky historical marker
4/10 mile
1005
252
5.6
1013
96
sign: "Bon Ami Baptist Church"
363
3.9
1.1
KIRBYVILLE
1.3
6.8
82
82
SILSBEE 32 | 96 | 1013

155

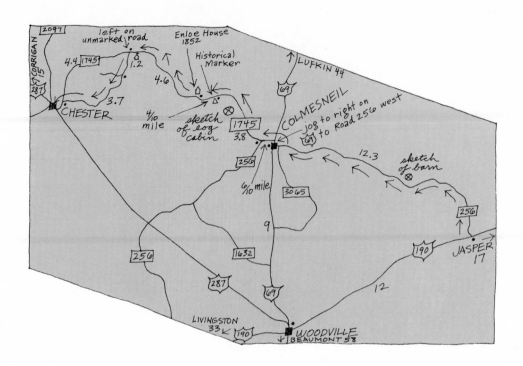

The road through Colmesneil

    After drawing the handsome old barn opposite,
I sketched an old log house in a setting of
post oak, red oak, and pine. The adze work
    and ax work on it were "straight, as if
it were sawed," according to John Sturrock,
who had partially restored the tiny dwelling.

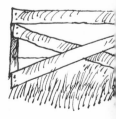

W W Ranch barn

157

Sturrock's
log cabin

159

San Augustine to Hemphill

Christ Church Episcopal, 1869, is a strongly braced post-and-beam structure on a tree-lined street (South Ayish near Market Street) in San Augustine.

The bell tower was added in 1891 to this well-preserved, historic church, making it a pleasing structure to look at, indeed.

SAN AUGUSTINE
147
2213
21
↓ BRONSON
8.5

(farmland, pasture and forest)

FORD'S CORNER
21 / GENEVA 5.8
1
4.1
MILAM 8.1 →
103
• 0.8

(cows, old barns, long chicken houses)
1592 5.3
2784

2.5

BRONSON ← 8.9
1592
184
2
184

HEMPHILL

Christ Church Episcopal Church, 1869

160

Just off the old town square in Hemphill is the 1916 Hotel Williams. The pin oak planted by Sim Williams is pictured here, but the garden that Mrs. Williams once kept and the full dining rooms are only an old-timer's memory.

In earlier days, businessmen would sit awhile in rockers on the front porch before going in to lunch.

Hotel Williams, Hemphill

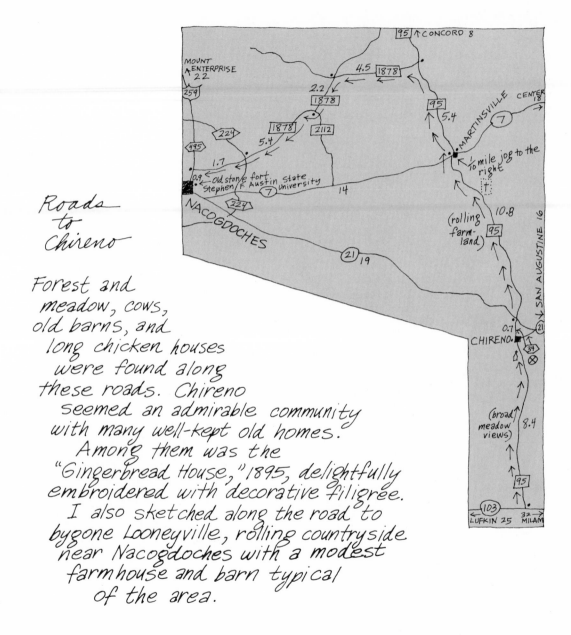

Roads
to
Chireno

Forest and
meadow, cows,
old barns, and
long chicken houses
were found along
these roads. Chireno
seemed an admirable community
with many well-kept old homes.
Among them was the
"Gingerbread House," 1895, delightfully
embroidered with decorative filigree.
I also sketched along the road to
bygone Looneyville, rolling countryside
near Nacogdoches with a modest
farmhouse and barn typical
of the area.

The Gingerbread House, Chireno

165

along the road
to Looneyville

166

167

Farm road to Henderson

A jog off the main back road took me to a view of the plantation home of Julien Devereaux, called Monte Verdi, built in the mid-1840s. At that time there were slaves and 10,000 acres of land to the plantation.

A green, gently undulating plain sprinkled with cheery yellow ragwort fronted the old mansion. Cows mooed, birds sang, and the leaves of the trees rustled in the wind.

Monte Verdi plantation home

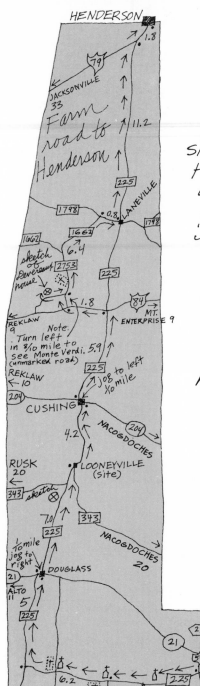

The road through Noonday to Jefferson

There was a display of register signatures in the lobby of the old Excelsior Hotel in Jefferson. I saw Grant's signature, with the abbreviation "Gnl" for "General"; Gould's, with a jay bird pictured in lieu of "Jay"; and that of former president Rutherford B. Hayes.

I drew the old synagogue, which is now the location of the Jefferson Playhouse. The first weekend of May, a play depicting a sensational murder that occurred in the early days is held here during the annual Jefferson Historical Pilgrimage.

The Jessie Allen Wise Garden Club owns both the hotel and the former synagogue and keeps them in good repair.

This was an east Texas town of great historical importance to see. Staying at Excelsior Hotel and having breakfast in the sunlit patio were highlights of my travels in Texas.

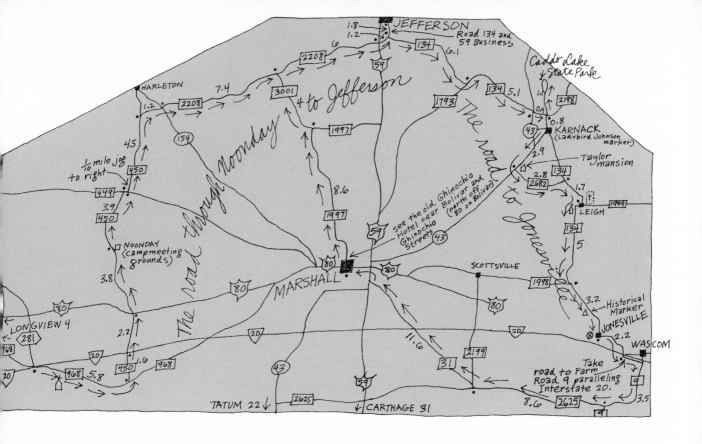

The map contains the following labels and route markers:

- 1.8 — JEFFERSON
- 1.2
- Road 134 and 59 Business
- 2208 — .6
- 134
- 6.1
- 59
- Caddo Lake State Park
- 7.4 — HARLETON
- 3001
- 4 to Jefferson
- 134 — 5.1
- 1793
- The road to Karnack
- 1.1 — 2198
- .4
- 1.2 — 2208
- 1997
- 43 — 0.8 — KARNACK (Ladybird Johnson marker)
- 154
- 2.9
- Taylor mansion
- 4.5
- The road through Noonday
- 2.8 — 134
- 2682 — 1.7
- 1/10 mile jog to right
- 450
- 8.6
- 1999 — LEIGH
- 449
- 1997
- 134
- 3.9
- 450
- 59
- See the old Ghinochio Hotel near Bolivar and Ghinochio Streets (north off 80 on Bolivar).
- 43
- The road to Jonesville
- 5
- NOONDAY (campmeeting grounds)
- 80 — MARSHALL
- 80
- SCOTTSVILLE
- 1998
- 3.8
- 3.2 — Historical Marker
- 80
- 80
- JONESVILLE
- LONGVIEW 4
- 281
- 2.2
- 80
- 20
- 80
- 2.2 — WASCOM
- 968
- 20
- 11.6
- 20
- Take road to Farm Road 9 paralleling Interstate 20.
- 20
- 968 — 5.8 — 450 — .6 — 968
- 43
- 59
- 31 — 2199
- 9
- 8.6 — 2625 — 3.5
- TATUM 22
- 2625
- CARTHAGE 31
- 4

Gnl Grant   Washington City

Gould   New York City

R. B. Hayes.   Washington D.C.

Signatures at Excelsior Hotel, Jefferson

The Jefferson Playhouse

173

The road to Jonesville

The old post office occupies one little corner in the incredible T.C. Lindsey and Company store at Jonesville. T.C. Lindsey told me that in the old days the top "open" boxes of the post office were for the poor folks and the bottom "locked" boxes for the richer ones. The original post office isn't used any more but is kept on display — as are a thousand and one items in this most colorful Texas store.

The country store in Jonesville

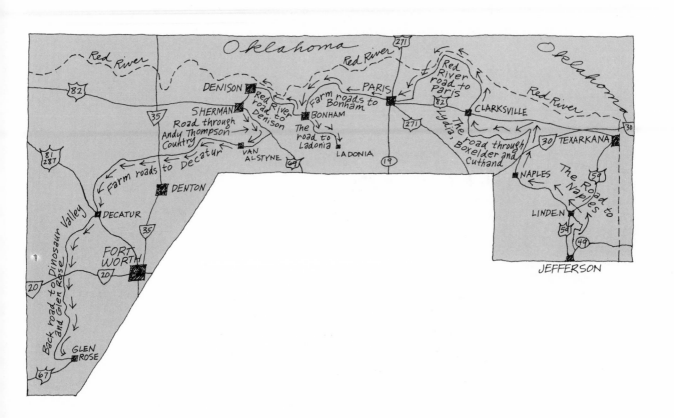

Northern Texas

Some back roads followed the Red River along the northern Texas border. I sketched a white spider-lily to the tune of croaking frogs and with the feeling of being deep in the country. Bird sounds filled the air around me. Purple prairie clover bloomed in abundance, as did Indian paintbrush and bright blue spiderwort.

In northwestern Texas, I descended into the color-filled gorge that is the Palo Duro Canyon for a different kind of visual experience.

Pincushion Daisy

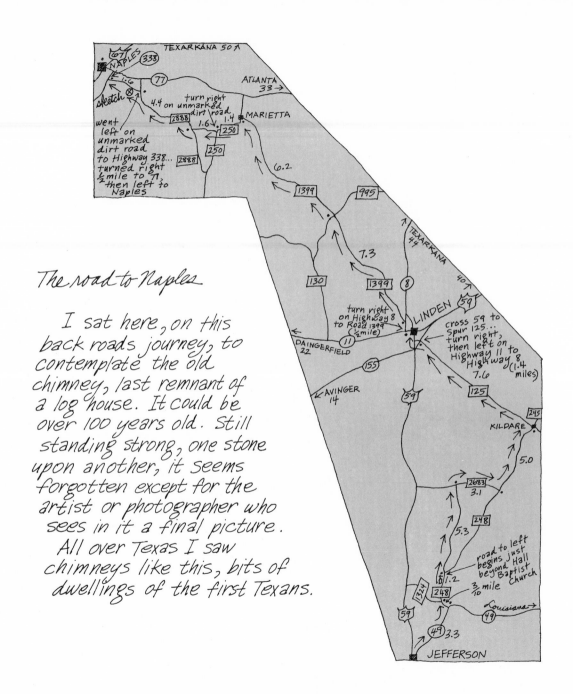

The road to Naples

I sat here, on this back roads journey, to contemplate the old chimney, last remnant of a log house. It could be over 100 years old. Still standing strong, one stone upon another, it seems forgotten except for the artist or photographer who sees in it a final picture.

All over Texas I saw chimneys like this, bits of dwellings of the first Texans.

The chimney

The road through Lydia,
Boxelder, and Cuthand

In spring this trip is through rolling, green farmland. Here I sketched another Texas relic, the rapidly disappearing and nearly extinct general store and gas-pump.

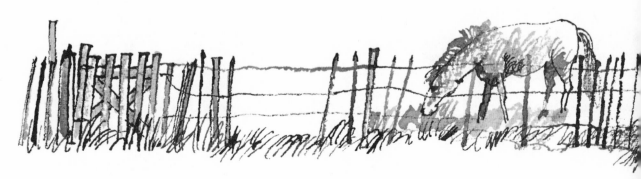

General store and gas pump near Cuthand

181

The Red River County Courthouse tower thrusts high above the town of Clarksville. It is a yellow stone building of massive proportions, built in 1885. At one time, the Donoho Hotel and Stage Stand stood opposite the first courthouse, and stagecoaches left every two days to Paris, Dallas, and Waxahachie. Every Monday, Wednesday, and Friday they traveled to Jefferson and Daingerfield.

CLARKSVILLE

sketch of courthouse

909

910

82

10.4

910

412

1487

CUTHAND 3.6

sketch of old store

1487

2.2

5.5

412

BOXELDER

9.4

ANNONA 7.6

44

911

LYDIA

44

5.1

AVERY 7.6

3165

HODGSON

3.1

44

DE KALB

259

1/10 mile

992

2.1

3/10 mile

3/10 mile

259

44

NAPLES 30

Red River
County
Courthouse,
Clarksville

183

Red River Road to Paris

I sketched Slate Rock Church across an immense grassy pastureland sprinkled with buttercups. On the left you can see people rounding up a cow that had somehow gotten onto the road.

A historical marker along Red River Road records where Sam Houston first set foot in Texas. This was at the old Jonesboro Crossing, which had opened as early as 1814 to the first North American settlers.

Slate Rock Church

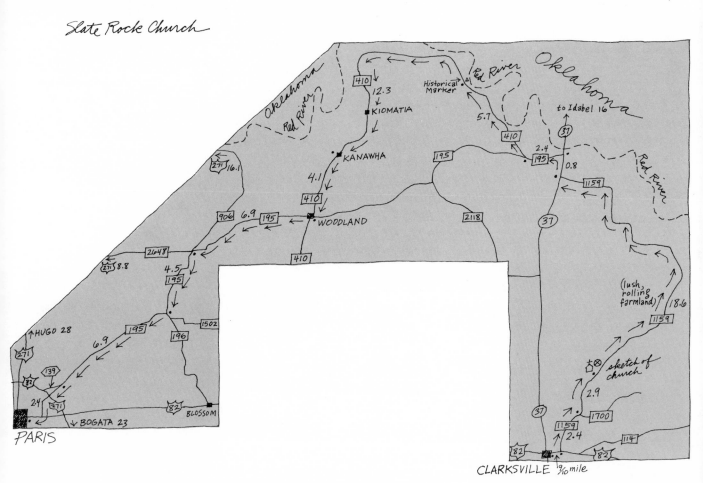

185

Farm roads to Bonham

Bonham was Sam Rayburn's hometown. He was speaker of the United States House of Representatives longer than any other legislator in our history.

You can see his former home and visit the Sam Rayburn Memorial Library, a gracious edifice of white Georgia marble. It contains an exact replica of "Mister Sam's" U.S. Capitol office and his mementos. Nearby is another replica, one of Fort Inglish, an 1837 log blockhouse built to protect the then-new town of Bonham.

Old Fort Inglish and the Sam Rayburn Library

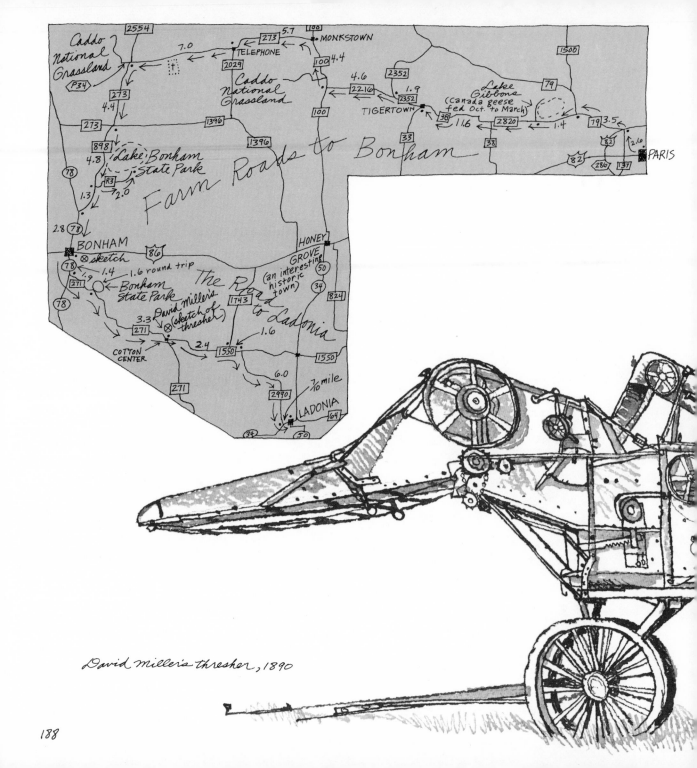

Farm Roads to Bonham

The Road to Ladonia

2554
Caddo National Grassland
P34
273
4.4
273
898
4.8
Lake Bonham State Park
R3
1.3
2.0
2.8 78
BONHAM
⊗ sketch
86
78
.9
1.4 — 1.6 round trip
271
Bonham State Park
78
3.3 David Miller's (sketch of thresher) ⊗
271
COTTON CENTER
271
1.6
2.4
1550
6.0
2990
7/10 mile
34
LADONIA
64
50

7.0
273 5.7
MONKSTOWN 100
TELEPHONE
2029
100 4.4
Caddo National Grassland
4.6
2352
2216
1.9
2352
Lake Gibbons (canada geese fed Oct. to March)
79
1500
1396
TIGERTOWN
36
11.6
2820
1.4
79 3.5
79
1.9
82
2.6
PARIS
1396
33
38
82
286
137

1743
34
824
HONEY GROVE (an interesting historic town)
50
1550
1550

David Miller's thresher, 1890

188

The road to Ladonia

In David Miller's pasture there was a grand display of horse-drawn equipment gathered from farms in Texas, Tennessee, Arkansas, and Louisiana. From his outdoor museum I selected an old 1890 thresher to draw.

It looked somewhat like a disproportionate, mechanical duck.

Ladonia had many Victorian style homes, a town square, and a number of turn-of-the-century brick buildings.

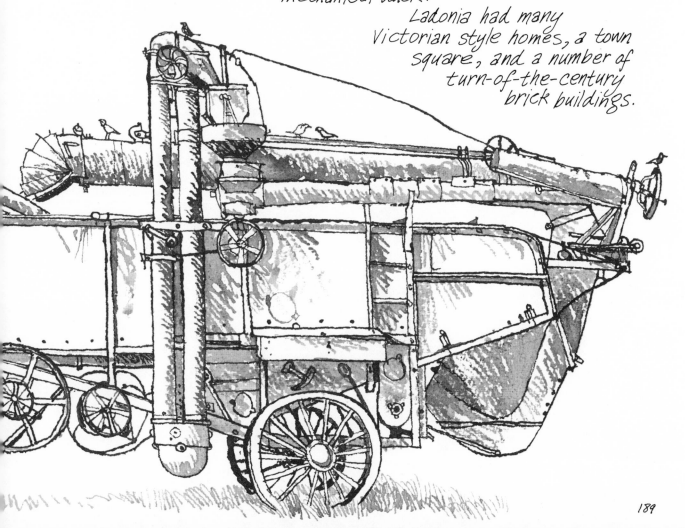

190   Butter
       daisy

Flutter
mill

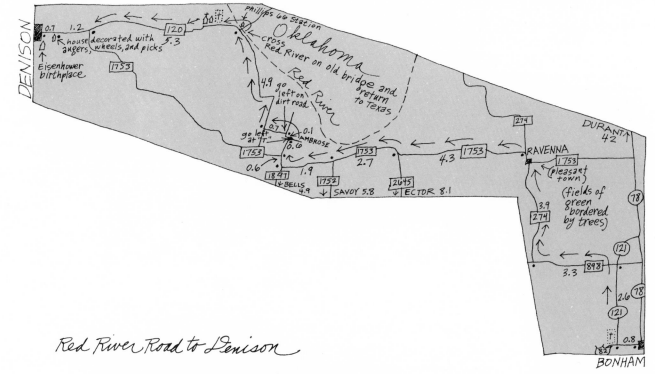

Red River Road to Denison

     There were several antique bridges
to rumble over on this trip. One spanned the
Red River itself into Oklahoma, with a
marvelous view of the big stream.
     The lively town of Denison began its career
as a stop on the Butterfield overland mail route in 1858.
             Here, open to the public, is the
birthplace of Dwight D. Eisenhower, a two-story, white
frame house at 208 East Day Street.

Road through Andy
Thompson country

Local people told me
that Andy Thompson traveled
with Davy Crockett, but when
Davy went to the Alamo, Andy
stayed and settled this
territory.

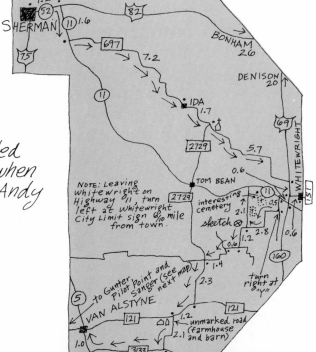

NOTE: Leaving
whitewright on
Highway 11, turn
left at whitewright
City Limit sign 6/10 mile
from town.

192

Reverend Isaac Teague's place

Here I visited an interesting cemetery on a rise of land containing the graves of Texas's first settlers, people born as early as 1806.

My sketch was of Reverend Isaac Teague's log house and the tree under which he performed marriages for most of the people in the township.

Farther along, I enjoyed exploring the back streets of Van Alstyne, Gunter, Pilot Point, and Sanger.

Farm roads to Decatur

go left at "Y"
0.9
1.0
go left at "Y" (dirt road)
1.0
455
51
730
GREENWOOD
↑ GAINESVILLE 25
Historical marker
GAINESVILLE 19 ↑
35
sketch
⊗
138
2450
3.5
455
0.4
4.4
3.7
51
2.5
SLIDELL
5.7
3.7
1204
Δ
3 455
SANGER
210
12.7
51
1173
DENTON 14 ↓
DECATUR
380

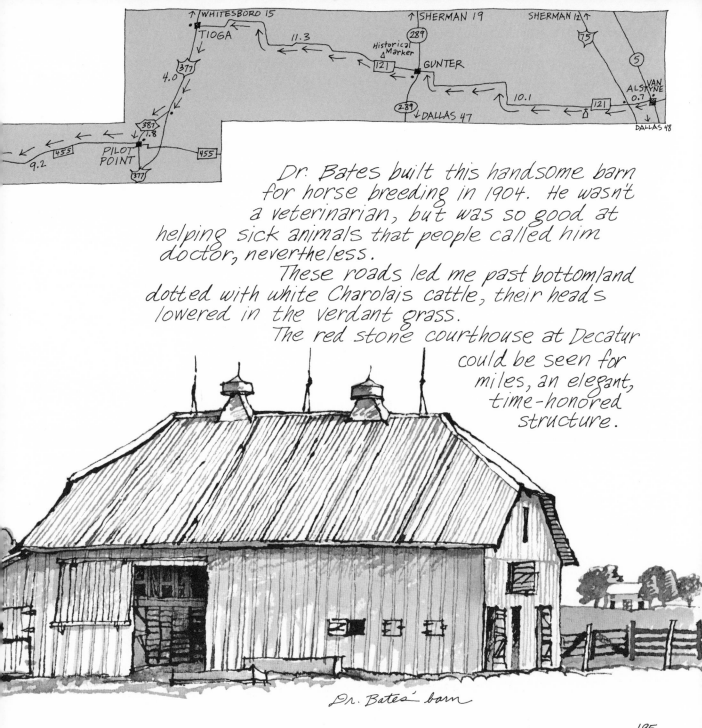

Dr. Bates built this handsome barn
for horse breeding in 1904. He wasn't
a veterinarian, but was so good at
helping sick animals that people called him
doctor, nevertheless.

These roads led me past bottomland
dotted with white Charolais cattle, their heads
lowered in the verdant grass.

The red stone courthouse at Decatur
could be seen for
miles, an elegant,
time-honored
structure.

Dr. Bates' barn

Back road to Dinosaur Valley and Glen Rose

The log cabin I sketched in the fascinating
town of Granbury (at South Baker and West Bridge
streets) had been moved from eight miles away.
It was once the Panter Branch Post Office,
owned by a gentleman named Elmore Snider.

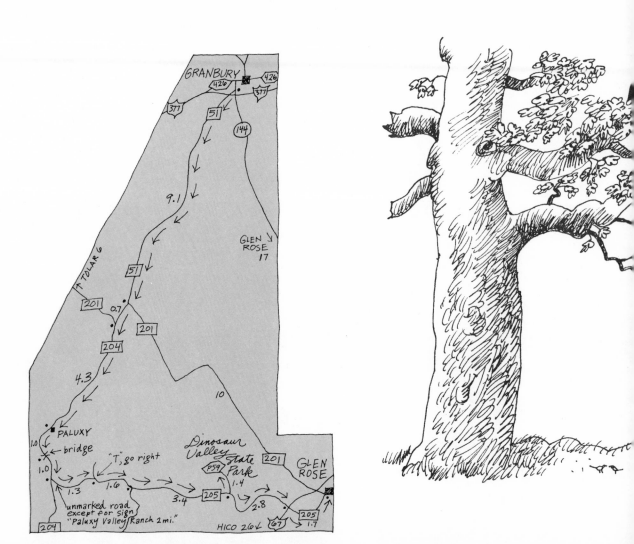

GRANBURY
426
426
377
377
51
144
9.1
GLEN
ROSE
17
↑ TOLAR 6
51
201
0.7
201
204
4.3
10
PALUXY
1.0
bridge
"T", go right
1.0
Dinosaur
Valley
State
Park
201
GLEN
ROSE
1.3
1.6
P59
1.4
3.4
205
2.8
205
1.7
unmarked road
except for sign
"Paluxy Valley Ranch 2 mi."
204
HICO 26 ↓
67

1960

On the way to Dinosaur Valley I saw jackrabbits loping through the brush alongside the road. This route was a pleasant and unusual approach to the unique valley where the first sauropod tracks were discovered. Other tracks were of duckbilled dinosaurs and theropods.

Glen Rose on the Paluxy River proved a neat and charming village to visit nearby.

Panter Branch
Post Office,
Granbury

Capitol Peak, Palo Duro Canyon

198

199

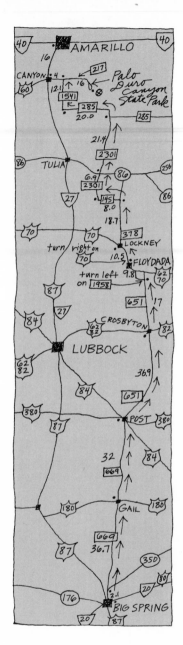

Roads to Palo Duro Canyon

On these roads across the prairie of the Texas Panhandle, I viewed vast acreages of plowed red earth, farms and windmills, buttes and distant mountains, crop-textured fields, grazing cows, big blue skies, and farmers waving from tractors — all ending in the great Palo Duro Canyon.

I hiked a bit to draw Capitol Peak, red ochre and purple in the sunlight.

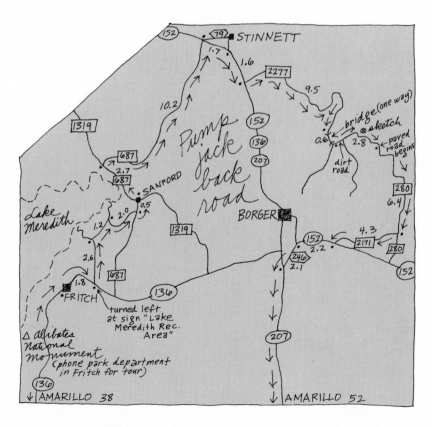

Pump jack back road

This was windswept prairie and canyonland country, replete with hundreds of pump jacks and oily smells. The most significant part of the journey was a ride over a one-half mile one-way bridge spanning the meanderings of the sometimes flowing Canadian River.

Alibates National Monument, near Fritch, contains quarries mined by Indians for flint as long as 10,000 years ago.

Thoughts while traveling

Being an enthusiast for back road travel, I have a wish that back roads be honored. Let them be narrow and winding, even bumpy and slow-going. I will take the time, then, to know and appreciate the beauty of the land, the flowers, the animals, the birds, and the sky.

As you may have noticed, I don't leave a lot of room for text in my book. I've always felt that pictures can speak volumes and the seeing of an object can be even more informative than trying to describe it in words.

Upon reaching towns, I drove the back streets. Local maps, the chamber of commerce, or the historical society were helpful, as were townspeople also in guiding me to the interesting features of a community.

I stay off of private property unless permission is given to enter. I consider this very important. Of course, I mean no harm but merely come to look and draw. I take nothing from the landscape. Only litter do I carry away with me.

203

Epilogue

What I hope I have done in this book, in addition to drawing places and things for your pleasure, is to lead you onto roads that you would not otherwise have taken. I would wish for you to see the world each day afresh in a new way. I hope, too, that your interest will be piqued enough for you to plan other back road trips. I could lead you only to some of the beautiful places in Texas. There are so many more to be discovered by you.

See the art box in the picture on the right? There it lies by the side of the road. In the spring it fell off the running board of my pickup truck where I had absent-mindedly placed it. My son had crafted the box for me, and it contained precious pens, brushes, inks and a valued pair of eyeglasses. I never saw it again until the box was found in late summer and shipped to me by a considerate Texan. I wish to thank Fred Ende of Greenville for his kindness.